Ridicula

by

Adam Altman

© Copyright 2018, Adam Altman

All Rights Reserved.

No part of this book may be reproduced, stored in a retrieval system, or transmitted by any means, electronic, mechanical, photocopying, recording, or otherwise, without written permission from the author.

ISBN: 978-1-64255-396-3

Maude pulled up in her truck. "We gotta be going," Maude spoke hurriedly through the window and opened the passenger's side door for him. Anxiety was apparent in her brutish face.

He got in without much thought. If he had been thinking, he would have realized that he wasn't involved in the trouble that Maude had likely gotten into, that he had no reason to go with her, and that he was hungry; Maude had no food, not even jerky, in the truck. And if he had stayed in Lake Tahoe longer, he could have avoided everything that was about to happen. But Hippie always seemed to find himself in interesting situations. So why should this be any different?

Maude peeled out with Hippie in tow. Where they were going now, he couldn't guess. He knew, however, that he'd be in Wyoming eventually.

He always ended up there.

Acknowledgement

This dedication is for the large list of people who made this book possible. You know who you are.

Ridicula (definitions by point of view)

1) Ridiculous to most but par for the course for the selected few—Hippie.

2) Extremely ridiculous but somehow plausible—George Cramwell.

3) Well beyond ridiculous, approaching stupidity and insanity; mostly associated with humans—Freckles.

4) Spanish word for ridiculous but without the accent mark.

Contents

Prologue 1
Chapter 1: A Modern Hippie 3
Chapter 2: Trying to Avoid the Inevitable 9
Chapter 3: Freckles 19
Chapter 4: Mistaken Identity 23
Chapter 5: A Glut of SUVs 27
Chapter 6: The Chase and the Capture 35
Chapter 7: Waterskiing 101 41
Chapter 8: Faulkner 49
Chapter 9: This One's for the Birds 57
Chapter 10: Following Each Other 63
Chapter 11: The Send Button 69
Chapter 12: The Hat and the Cat 81
Chapter 13: A Soap Altercation 87
Chapter 14: Inside a Jules Verne Novel 95
Chapter 15: Before the Big Day 107
Chapter 16: The Ranger 113
Chapter 17: Bloodshedder 123
Chapter 18: The Dawn of Reckoning 131
Chapter 19: The Rich and the Obsessed 137
Chapter 20: Bloodshedder's Soulmate 143
Chapter 21: The Grand Fetcher Escapade:
　　　　　　The End of the Ultimate Chase 149
Chapter 22: Seventies or Eighties Music 153

Chapter 23: Bloodshot Love 161
Chapter 24: Doggy Joy 165
Chapter 25: Contemplation 169
Epilogue 173

Prologue

Dressed in camouflage brown clothes to blend in with the immediate semidesert surroundings, Carolyn investigated the situation at hand. Her subject was within sight, at least via binoculars. She watched anxiously even though she knew that he couldn't see her, and it was unlikely that he could recognize her in any case, nor could the one he was with. She was too far away, and twilight shadows covered her.

The two were walking down a dingy street—kind of a half-road, a dirt-nothing where weeds made up most of the road and where potholes caused flattened tires. She had seen many bad roads in places other than the crappy ones in New Jersey, where she grew up. This was one of those roads.

The stranger talking to her man looked like someone who may have been in the news forty years ago. He had a scraggly beard like a hippy, but somehow, he appeared more sophisticated. This was perhaps because of what he held, surely a product of excellent quality. Her man would want nothing other than the best.

She had never seen her man use drugs. That's not what he was about. That is probably why she saw sophistication in the other man, who was no drug dealer. He likely sold better quality material. Her man was often in the company of such men—those who looked shady but were of higher class. And being out together at twilight would make sense, for her incubus was a man of the night.

Just like she was a lady who preferred the night.

Her thoughts wandered. She began to think of her life as one big investigative news blogger, reporting about potential assailants but not making any big difference to the world. She was both the pursuer and the assailant, a victim of her desire. She wondered about her motive, for she was never clear about why she was doing what she was doing. She reasoned that it was because she has gone through life without him, the one who made her long existence worthwhile.

She had found him now and was certain he was the one. She had smelt him up close, and his scent was right. He had the allure, the blood, and the odor.

He fascinated her.

And he was gone. She had let her distracted thoughts overtake her long enough to lose focus, letting him disappear. The only human she saw now was his friend.

Damn!

Well, his friend would have to do. The hippy was her only lead now. And she was certain that he would eventually lead her back to the man Carolyn pursued.

Chapter 1
A Modern Hippie

The sun had just started to peek over the lip of the roof when Hippie awoke from his slumber. He lifted his head from the threadbare brown couch and breathed in the crisp air of the morning. Still groggy from sleep, he sat up to look at the leaves on the few trees whose height reached above him and studied the red rocks that formed the small hills of the terrain.

As he touched the tiles of the flat roof, he thought about the long trek he was going to embark on this lovely late summer day. His friends had kindly let him sleep on the couch on the roof of their house — the same couch he had brought up there the year before. Luckily, it didn't rain much in these parts, and the couch wasn't dilapidated enough for him to be forced to sleep elsewhere. It was rather comfortable, actually. He had spent nights in far worse surroundings.

He had enjoyed the comfort of the couch the last few days, but now it was time to say goodbye, take his belongings, and move on. He was positive he would be welcomed back in case he returned in the next few months. Knowing himself, it was certainly a possibility.

He stood up and edged his way to the peak of the roof. He looked down, realizing that it was easier to climb up the roof than to climb back down. He thought of jumping, but it was not a short leap, and he worried that he might land the wrong way and sprain his ankle. However, this was not as dangerous as compared to many other actions he had attempted in his life.

Without hesitating any longer, he jumped. He landed on the ground on his two feet, still standing. He raised his arms in triumph. Then he closed his eyes and murmured a silent 'thank you,' for his slightly aged body could not keep up with this way of life quite as well as ten years ago, although he remained in good shape and planned to stay that way.

Of course, the family that let him stay here were all gone. The parents were at work, and the kids had left for school. Why anyone would want to go to work was beyond him. What would they get out of it? Money? Stuff? Material things did not mean much in the scheme of real life, but most people seemed possessed by them. Deep down, though, he knew that even he had to work occasionally to make ends meet.

The family had left the door open for him. He walked in and took some time to pet and feed the cats and walk and feed the dog. They were friendly animals and he would miss them, as he always did when he left.

Before grabbing his small leather case that held most of his belongings, he wrote a note to the family to thank them for their hospitality and that he would try to keep in touch with them. He might be a hippy and a wanderer, but he was courteous about it.

Taking his case, he took the "Care" package from the refrigerator that this family always left him, turned off all the lights, and locked the door behind him. He was ready to embark on his next adventure.

As he waited at the side of the main road in town, he looked through his Care package. There really was not much to it, but it had some of his essentials: an apple, a power bar, a jar of wheat juice, a container of water, and of course, a few multipurpose vitamins. However, it was the two additional items that brought a smile to his face. The small bottle of niacin was a pleasure he did not often receive. Yes, when he tried some, he would itch and feel flushed for a few minutes, like a red marshmallow, with his heart beating fast, but it would all be worth it, for he always became more energetic and healthier after the initial side-effects wore off. The final item in his package was a bar of soap. The family he had just left knew that he preferred to be clean. He was a hippy, but hygiene was still important.

As he looked up, a truck pulled over in front of him. The stout woman behind the wheel waved for him to come over. This time, it looked like he wouldn't need to put his thumb up. It was certainly looking like a promising day. He walked over to the truck, and the big burly redneck type of woman cleared some space so that he could sit down. "Where are you off to?" she said in her gruff voice. She wasn't the most pleasant person to look at with her heavyset frame, rotten teeth, and somewhat manly mustache, but at the moment, Hippie didn't care. His next main stop would likely be at one of his girlfriend's places, where he could take in a prettier sight.

"Nebraska, not far from Omaha." He had decided which girlfriend would be best to see.

"That's a mighty long way. Do you know that you're in the Central Valley of California right now?" the woman said with a quick huff of a laugh as she began to drive again.

"Yes, I'm aware," Hippie said calmly. It wasn't the first time he would go on a trip such as this. He also wouldn't be surprised if he had to go through Wyoming again before heading back south towards Nebraska, but he was in no rush.

"Well, I'm heading to Lake Tahoe. Ski season is coming, and I've got some material to deliver. It's north of here and probably cool, but at least it's east and will get you on your way. Do you have a jacket? You might need one."

Hippie thought, *A motherly yet tough redneck—oh, this might work out well.*

After he nodded yes, the woman continued. "Well, is it a warm jacket? Cause I'll be continuing to head northeast after Lake Tahoe." Oh, yes, he was heading back to Wyoming! Maybe it was Wyoming of all places that was his true destination.

"Look, miss," Hippie started, "I don't own a heavy coat. Do you think I could really fit that type of jacket in my small case? Don't worry. I'll make do." Some people just didn't understand the way of the hippy. You must travel light. If there comes a time when you own too many heavy objects, you trade some of them for something smaller or just give them away. You can even sell them at a fair price, of course. This hippy was not just thumbs, peace, and love.

The woman trucker was now driving onto Route 5. Since she was heading towards Lake Tahoe, they would only be a short time on the dreaded highway. Hippie hated most highways — too many cars with the people inside them not caring about anything but getting from one place to another. Since there was too much traffic anyway, people couldn't go as fast as they wanted, so they blew their horns, cut off other drivers, and just acted like fools. Hippie often wondered where everybody was going so fast — probably home or work. Well, he guessed that home would be okay if relaxation was on their minds or the love of their significant other. *But work? Oh, not that unproductive, nothing to do with reality boss man work! Real work is fine if it's to the ends of helping people, surviving, or creating something worthwhile. But most jobs are not real, just an empty means to make tiny bits of money and with little to no gratification.*

After obliterating work from his mind, Hippie decided that he should become chummy with his host driver. After all, they were going to spend many hours together. "So, ma'am, I never caught your name."

"Maude. And yours?"

"Aspen—named after the tree and the huge Dodge seventies car, not these new pieces of crap cars—but no one really calls me by that name. As a matter of fact, usually no one calls me by any one name. When necessary, some of my buddies call me Hippie, although I have no idea why," he said with his wry smile.

The woman did not see that smile, so she took his remark seriously, replying, "Your hair, man. Your hair." Then, after a quick look in his direction, she continued, "And I'm sure you'll want a little of the stash I have. Help yourself—but don't take too much."

"What? You have extra vitamins you can spare?" He knew what she meant but wanted to see her reaction.

He got what he expected. "No, man. Pot, of course," she said, amazed, still not catching on to his humor.

After he shook his head to decline, Maude laughed for a moment. "What kind of hippy are you anyway?"

"That's what I'm trying to tell you. I'm not your ordinary, pot-smoking, free-lovin', peaceful hippy," Hippie said laughing, and then clarified, "Oh, well, maybe I'm peaceful and a bit free-lovin', but I don't believe in most drugs. Vitamins will do just fine for me."

Hippie then hesitated a moment before asking for his drug of choice. "Got any beer?"

At that, Maude gave one big hoot of laughter that made her mustache look more hideous. Her shirt popped out of her pants to show her bulky stomach for a moment. That ugly mix nauseated

Hippie more than it should have. After all, he was used to bad-looking women and had slept with a few over the years. He knew why he was disgusted, though, remembering all his shenanigans with his beer and the round women phase of his life.

"Well, do you got any beer?" he couldn't help repeating.

Maude renewed her low-pitched hoot, but this time, it became many hoots of laughter. She even veered off the highway for a moment in her display of glee. Well, at least this trip was getting off to a rollicking start. Hopefully, they would venture into the land of half streets, and then the craziness might really begin.

And this made Hippie think of last month when George had visited him at the place where they had first met and became friends—

Chapter 2
Trying to Avoid the Inevitable

"The road was called 16 ½ street," George Cramwell said and then writing it out on a bar napkin. "The ½ was a fraction, not a decimal." George Cramwell finished writing the mixed number. "And the sign didn't even point to any road. There was only grass there. Absurd. What did they do? Call it a half street cause the road wasn't finished yet?" George shook his head and then continued. "That wasn't the only occurrence of this half street phenomenon. The streets went all the way up to 32 ½ street or maybe even higher." George continued writing whole numbers on the napkin.

Kenny Dunz had heard this story a few times before, so he just tuned out George and let him continue his ridiculous rant. Maybe George was so enthralled with his story because it took place outside of New York City, where he rarely ventured.

No matter. Right now, Kenny only had the inclination to scope out the scene.

With a Molson in hand, he looked around the crowded bar but did not see anyone he knew. That was not a problem, though. He could always find a cute girl to talk to, but no one immediately caught his attention until a group of women around his age walked through the front door. *Not bad. Not bad at all*, he thought.

But then he saw the last woman to walk in. He could not mistake the long brunette hair that hung past her ass, dark brown sinister eyes, and an indecent smile, as though she were a naughty princess entering the tavern on a dare.

Jade had come to ruin the evening.

Kenny proceeded to slam his Molson down in distaste. Beer and scoping out women were not important for Kenny now.

His first concern was to avoid a bad scene. George could not see Jade or something miserable would happen. At best, they would avoid talking or only say a quick hello, but later, George would wind up talking Kenny's ear off with what-ifs and melancholy self-pity. That would be bad. But if Jade and George got into another awkward conversation, argument, or even a "healthy" talk, it would wind up much worse. No, Kenny would not allow that to happen.

"You know that there was even a 15 ¾ street? I thought I was going nuts when I saw that, especially cause the town was called: Madera. It was a 'mad era' alright," George said to the bartender, who was feigning interest and laughter while serving drinks to his other thirsty patrons.

Kenny tapped George on the shoulder. "Let's go. It's getting stuffy in here. No good chicks around anyway. Let's go to the Shaking Tree. There should be some good music there."

"Well, okay. But let me finish my story first," George replied. He always had to finish his stories.

"But you're only at the part about 15 ¾ street. You haven't even gotten to the part about swerving off the main highway at the grass base at 13 ½ street and getting help from Hippie," Kenny said in desperation. Jade might have already seen them. "And the bartender's busy anyway."

"Bob wants to hear the rest," George was saying as Kenny hurriedly looked around him. He quickly found Jade heading toward the bar. *Shit!* Kenny thought. *And I think she's seen me. Shit! Shit!*

He ran over to intercept her. Hopefully she hadn't seen George yet, and luckily, George had gone back to telling the bartender his whacked-out story.

"Oh, Kenny. How are you?" Jade said, using what she thought was her winning smile on him as he approached. Her smile was as convincing as the best of actresses, but Kenny knew better. Her smile repelled him. She had suckered so many men to do her will—and then discarded them like *Survivor* castoffs.

"I'm doing fine," he said with what he hoped was a convincing smile. He knew he had to act as sincere as possible so that she would not dismiss him too quickly. "It's great to see you," he continued with inner disgust. "We haven't seen each other in a while. How's everything with you? And who are your divine friends?"

At first, Jade looked at him strangely. *I guess she wasn't expecting me to take too much interest in her and her friends.* But then she gave him another smile and blinked her eyes alluringly. *Oh, jeez. Does she ever stop? Now she's trying to entice me with her eyes.*

"This is my friend Jen," Jade was saying, still smiling. "And this is Kim and Maria...."

"How about I buy all you ladies a drink?" he said, politely interrupting her.

"Well, how thoughtful of you." This time it was Maria talking.

"How does a Malibu sound?" Kenny asked Maria attentively and then thought to include Jade. "I know you like the pineapple ones, Jade. I'll get you each one."

"Yes, yes, that is my favorite," Jade replied, and Maria remained silent. "Do you have any friends with you that would like to join us?"

"Ahh, well." *Think fast. Come on, Kenny. Think fast. Got it!* "Ahh, I just came to visit my friend Bob, the bartender. I guess you found me out. He gives me really good deals on the drinks."

Jade did not reply right away. *She's probably thinking about how much bullshit I'm spouting.* She didn't trust too many people, so she had to examine everything.

Luckily, Maria spoke up for her. "Thank you. We'll wait for you at the table." Jade looked at her a moment. Then she shrugged her shoulders and followed Maria and the rest of her friends.

Kenny stood there for a minute, trying to think of what he should do next. Then he walked back towards the bar and saw that George was no longer there. *Shit!*

"Where'd my friend go?" he asked the bartender when he came around to take his order.

"Not sure. He hadn't even finished his story. He was talking about some tractor chasing his car through the grass heading towards 13 ½ street, but then he just got up and took off. He didn't look too well though. He's probably in the bathroom. Now, what will it be?"

"Four Malibus with pineapple juice. To go," he added, looking everywhere anxiously.

"To go? We're not in the Caribbean, and we don't serve umbrellas in our drinks. Not even when you order sissy drinks." The bartender usually displayed hospitality, but he probably had not liked how

Kenny had left him to his own devices instead of taking George and his lame story away from the bar.

"How much?" Kenny asked, implying by his tone that he hadn't realized that the bartender was becoming irritated by George's tale.

"Fifty-six dollars!" *Was the bartender overcharging him? No, it was just those damned city prices.*

"Fourteen-dollars apiece for sissy drinks! Damn, what is this bar coming to?" replied Kenny and handed the bartender three twenties, hoping to make amends for the bartender listening to George's story by leaving the four-dollar tip.

As the bartender went to make the drinks, Kenny began to walk towards the bathroom when he was tapped on the shoulder. He whirled around to see Maria standing before him. "Just wanted to see if you needed any help bringing back the drinks."

"Umm, well, ah, thanks," Kenny said, noticing for the umpteenth time tonight about how well-shaped her little figure was.

"So how do you know Jade?" she asked.

"Ah—umm," Kenny replied in such a manner that made a pimple-faced nerdy teenager sound suave. Finally, Kenny was able to say three real words. "From a friend."

"And that's him coming toward you?"

"Kenny, I didn't know you knew Maria," George said when he reached them.

"Oh, hi George. I didn't recognize you at first." Maria sounded sincere, but she looked around as if she were paranoid. Then she smiled and put her arm around George. "You know, Jade should be at the bar down the road. Maybe we should go over there. You coming, Kenny?" And she winked at him, discreetly.

Kenny was flabbergasted at first, but then realized that Maria was trying to get George out of there before he saw Jade. He guessed she knew something about the situation. "I'll join you both there soon."

Before George could say anything, Maria nearly pushed him forward, away from where Jade sat and led him through the crowd and out the door. Soon after, the bartender came back with the drinks. As he reached for the drinks, Jade came from behind and grabbed two of them. "I saw Maria leave with some guy. She's a quick worker, isn't she?"

"She sure is," Kenny Dunz replied, relieved that she hadn't immediately recognized George from such a distance.

Maria Nova had never felt comfortable at bars. Nor dance clubs. Nor weddings. Nor large house parties. Nor most other social gatherings where she didn't know the majority of people there. She enjoyed the company of a few close-knit friends rather than constantly meeting new people. She would rather go to a restaurant or movie or even put on those odorous rental shoes at a bowling alley as long as she was with friends she trusted.

Now, however, she was with George Cramwell, whose company might be suspect. Yes, she was acquainted with him through Jade, so he was not a complete stranger. But what did she really know about him?

George was Jade's on-and-off-again "boyfriend," currently off, and maybe this time, it would be permanent. Jade had had enough of his pandering to her every whim, putting her on a pedestal that she could never hope to attain. He was courteous and often helpful, but sometimes a girl just wanted to order her own coffee, see a movie with the gals, or have a little alone time. George didn't have to be there ALL the time. She had tried to tell him this, but he wouldn't listen. Sometimes she would say that she needed some alone time to think about things, but he claimed that that would not be good for their relationship. To some degree, he had a point. Not giving her this time, however, only made things worse. He became even more clingy. Thus, Jade had no choice but to break up with him yet again.

At least that was what Jade had told Maria. Although it sounded possible, Maria doubted the truth of it.

In any case, Maria had not wanted a scene so had gotten him out of the bar before he'd seen Jade. And in all truth, she had not much wanted to be there anyway. When they got to the next bar, she had checked to be sure that Jade had not somehow made her way there and then let George have a look. Now they were trying to hail a cab to their prospective apartments. They lived only a few blocks away from each other: she on Twenty-Seventh and Lex and he on Thirty-Third and Third.

No cabs drove by, so Maria became antsy. She wanted to go home; she had had enough of being out on the town.

George must have noticed her mood and said, "I'll call my cab."

"My cab?" Maria questioned, thinking that she had misheard.

"Yeah, my grandma owned a cab company," George announced with some pride.

"Owned?"

"Uh-huh. It's not like we sold the company, though. It's just that we no longer use it as a business. Still have some working cabs though."

"Then call Grandma and get us a taxi." She hoped she didn't sound too demanding, but the temperature was decreasing rapidly, and her antsiness was making her miserable.

"Grandma doesn't live here. She moved away from the city more than ten years ago, but the cabs are still around." George began to fidget, as if he were starting a Zumba routine with his fingers and toes outstretched and flexing. What was that about? Would he soon be breaking to the beat of "Greased Lightning"? She hoped her own antsy behavior didn't look like that.

"Then how are you to call a taxi?" Maria asked.

"Bobarino will come. You'll see." He pressed a button on his key ring. A flash of red, yellow, and green light displayed, like a disco ball emanating from a traffic light. Then some music played. To Maria, it sounded like a muzak version of "Greased Lightning." *Go figure.*

"What are you doing?" Maria had just about enough of this. No wonder Jade had dumped him. He was acting stranger each passing moment.

"I'm calling my buddy, Bobarino," George replied as he shook his hands in rhythm with the muzak.

Maria looked around. Were other people seeing this? When she saw a couple staring at them from across the street, she grimaced, embarrassed. "Will you please turn that off?"

"Not till I know that Bobarino got my call and received the GPS signal." Then came a loud beep. "Oh, he just got it," and George turned the muzak off.

"How far is he? When will he be here?" Maria was usually the patient type, but she had been reluctant to go out in the first place, had done nothing but barhopped and wandered, and now felt exhausted. Plus, she only stayed with George so that she would not be alone on a Saturday night. She half-wondered where Jade had gone but was too tired to truly care.

George did not need to answer her, because he saw a taxicab down the street. Or was it just a coughing muffler and an engine belching smoke with a burnt smell? When Maria finally saw through the smoke, it wasn't a yellow cab in her sight. Instead, she witnessed a blue one with brown pinstripes and cracked windshield. Or were the pinstripes rust?

"Oh, Bobarino, that was record time," George was saying to the driver as he opened the creaking back door. "You make those other New York cabbies seem slow."

Already wary of traveling in a heap of junk that George called a cab, Maria was also not impressed with how Bobarino drove like a speed demon drag car racer. In the blink of an eye, the cab had stopped in front of them, but when she had last seen it, it was blocks away. Had he also sped through a red light?

"Let's go," George said to her after finishing his conversation with the driver.

She inched her way to where George had left the door open for her. She peeked in to see and smell monstrosities: Bobarino looked like a mustached Amazonian muscle head with scars laced across his face and arms and tattoos on his neck and yes, ears; the cushions of the so-called cab were punctured from knives, pitchforks, or spears; and the taxi's odor smelt like wet wolves in heat.

"What's the hold up? Hop in," George continued.

Maria Nova found herself getting in the cab, almost against her will, as if some magic wind was pushing her. And in any case, she did need to get home. "What the hell," she said as she closed the door and cozied into her seat. "It won't take long to get home."

Famous last words.

***

What was Kenny doing? Was that supposed to be a dance move? It looked more like Big Bird from Sesame Street tripping over his own talons and bouncing back up with his butt.

On the other hand, why would he be dancing in the street? Was he too drunk to care? Or was it that no one else paid him any attention? Jade—who preferred never to volunteer her last name—didn't really care, either. She had seen much in the dozen years she lived in Manhattan, a place where anything went on at night. For instance, she had once seen a man taking a dump on the sidewalk in the middle of Times Square, and people just walked past him as if he weren't there. Of course, he was homeless so seemed to disappear in the background. Nevertheless, he had done it, perhaps just to get noticed but without much success. Possibly Kenny was trying to get noticed too but was failing. And maybe her two friends, Kim and Jen, had left earlier in order to not witness Kenny's antics any longer.

Jade had always found that Kenny marched to the beat of his own drum. She kind of liked him for that. He worked for himself, selling over the Internet anything he could lay his hands on as well as creating web pages and the like for anyone who would pay him. He couldn't be making much money, but he had survived the ridiculous expenses of the city for many years now so had to be doing something right.

A Wall Street woman herself, Jade envied the free spirits of someone like Kenny. Stockbrokers did not have the reputation for anything but hard work and smart investing. At least, that could be said for an honest stockbroker. But smart investing is what had attracted her to the field, for in her youth, she was always interested in the trade market. She had secretly followed the stock market religiously in high school while also following the popular girl route: many boyfriends, average grades, and cheerleading. Eventually, however, the nerd in her had won out, and she had gone to business school.

"Look at me. I can fly!" Kenny was saying as he jumped about an inch off the ground.

"Bravo!" Jade replied. "You're Superman!"

Ridicula

But Superman jumped once too many times and landed on the curb, tripping over it and onto Christopher Street. At this time of night, he had seconds before the next cab came motoring down the street like an accelerated junked-up train, but Kenny had time to roll back toward the sidewalk. A half a second later, the cab stopped beside him, inches away from his face.

To Jade, though, the strangest thing about this whole episode was that the cabbie never honked his horn, like all obnoxious drivers in New York City do. Did this taxi driver actually care that he had almost hit a drunken idiot who thought he was Superman?

"Jade!" a familiar voice was calling to her from inside the cab. And then she recognized the vehicle as one of George's grandmother's cabs. It was just her luck for Kenny to fall in front of this particular cab. Was it just odd coincidence in this big city or had Kenny and George somehow set this up so that Jade had no choice but to talk to George? But how could that be the case? She must be overly paranoid again.

Then she heard a female voice. Maria was in the cab with him! "Let's get Kenny into the cab and get him home," she said, and Jade saw the cab door open, revealing her friend.

"I'm okay. I'm okay," Kenny said, standing and jumping erratically to his feet.

Having no real choice, Jade went with them to the cab, noticing that George had not come out to help, too. *Typical man!* she thought, although she knew George was not that sort.

As soon as she stepped into the cab, she sniffed the odor of smoked fish and body odor. No one had cleaned this taxi in months. Ugh! But maybe it wasn't the cab at all, because she recognized the driver, who was not the cleanest cabbie. "Oh, hi Bobarino."

"Long time, no see," Bobarino replied.

"Kenny's apartment please," said George. With a puff and a skid, Bobarino sped off before Jade had time even to shut the door, as she was the last one in.

But they would never make it to Kenny's or any of their homes again for quite some time.

Chapter 3
Freckles

Freckles awoke to the sound of the annoying cat scratching her kitty litter. *Just go already,* he thought, for Freckles was not the type of dog that wasted time finding his spots to pee. When he had to go, he went. Usually, he waited till he went outside, but that was it. These grounds were his terrain. He didn't have to show off his territory to anyone.

Before standing and scaring off the cat, he took a look at his awesome features, as he always did in the morning. That's why he slept near the mirror. Not that he was vain or anything.

The humans, however, had taken forever to leave his bed near the mirror. They had decided to bring the bed there only after he'd settled on the floor next to the mirror for several weeks. Finally, the humans had gotten the hint. His humans weren't the brightest bulbs in this doghouse.

As a matter of fact, his humans were so dimwitted that they had named him Freckles when he didn't have a single spot on his entire glorious body. What did they think? That he was a Dalmatian? Please! No, he was a Rottweiler. And proud of it!

Because he was a Rottweiler, he guessed, was why some visitors of this house could initially be afraid of him. Sure, he was large and stout and might scare off the cat a time or two, but he was no Doberman; he was as friendly as could be.

But the cat was even dumber than humans, so as soon as she was ready to go, Freckles leaped across the room until he reached the bathroom, both guarding the litter box and threatening the cat. She skirted away in a hurry, forgetting her need to potty. Freckles never needed to hurt the kitty nor would he ever, but frightening her could still entertain him. At least the cat was good for a few chuckles.

Oblivious to the cat racing down the hallway, away from her kitty litter, the elderly humans walked past Freckles, who stood smirking at the bathroom door. "Dara is coming over today. We got to tidy up," said the white-haired old man who sometimes didn't remember his own name.

"She isn't coming, Harrison," his balding wife Lana said, always reminding him of his name no matter if he needed reminding or not. "She isn't coming today or tomorrow, nor did she come last week."

"Will she be coming next Wednesday?" he asked seriously.

"No, Harrison," Lana stated without elaborating.

When they passed the bathroom door, Freckles proudly trotted behind them. Meanwhile, the cat was nowhere to be found.

"Have you seen Dara?" Harrison asked Freckles as he patted him on the head. Of course, he couldn't talk to the man, but this is what he would have said: *No, she hasn't been here in years. I was just a pup when she last stopped by. Yet, I remember. Why can't you?*

Freckles immediately regretted thinking these words. He was not being fair. The old man obviously missed his daughter and just wanted to see her again. Maybe Freckles could make that happen someday. After all, his ability to smell someone out was uncanny even after sniffing that object for only a half-second. He was just that good.

"Have you seen my bat?" Harrison went on to say, changing the subject or forgetting what he'd been saying. "I'm going to hit some tennis balls for our dog to fetch."

Our dog. Right! That's like saying that the cat isn't afraid of me.

"Are you sure you can handle that right now?" his wife asked in a very unassuming way.

"Of course, I can, Woman!" Harrison yelled back as if she had just asked him whether he could talk or not.

"I'm not your woman! I'm your wife. Keep saying that and I'll bat those tennis balls into your groin!"

Not taking any lip from his wife, Harrison went to her, shoved the palm of his hand to within centimeters of her nose, and shouted, "Stop!"

Meanwhile, Freckles sat down to enjoy the theatrics, tongue hanging from his mouth as if waiting for Harrison to find the tennis balls but actually just enjoying the show performed by the ridiculous humans. Once settled, he was in time to see Lana swipe her husband's hand away and begin scolding him.

"How dare you?" she retorted, not one to back down from anyone, let alone her husband. "I'm only watching out for your safety. You're not a spring chicken anymore, Harrison."

Freckles thought about finding a chicken to chase but then reconsidered. The humans were more entertaining than any chicken.

"I can hit a damned tennis ball. Now where's my bat?" Harrison looked around the vicinity as if his bat would suddenly appear in front of him.

"Check your closet. It's probably with the rest of your junk," Lana surrendered to his stubbornness but not without one more remark, "You're going to hurt your back. Mark my words."

Harrison harrumphed, dismissing her with the wave of his hand. He walked towards his closet where he kept most of his stuff that he couldn't bring himself to throw away. At least Freckles knew when a tennis ball had been chewed to the point of disuse. Harrison didn't seem to learn this trivial lesson. He couldn't distinguish new from relic, useful from unpractical, good junk from bad crap.

And sure enough, as soon as he opened the closet door, an old crusty glove fell from the packed upper shelf and smote him on the head, dust careening from both the glove and his hair. Afterward, the glove fell harmlessly to the floor.

Harrison sneezed one loud and powerful "Achew!" and then he followed the glove to the ground and clenched his lower back. "Sweetheart, I need help. My back!"

Watching from the nearby doorway and seeing that he was not seriously hurt, Lana couldn't help but laugh. "You didn't even make it outside or find the bat yet. Come here, my old husband. Give your wife a hug."

Harrison picked himself back up, stretching until he realized that his back was all right. He limped to his wife anyway, although he clearly wasn't injured. Freckles could tell because the man kept forgetting which leg it was that supposedly bothered him, not to mention that his original complaint was about his back. Thankfully, Harrison let the charade die in favor of hugging his wife and pecking her on the cheek. "I'm an old bumbling fool sometimes," he said.

"That's why I still love you, Harry," his wife replied, returning a kiss to his cheek.

Freckles stood up then. When the humans got lovey-dovey with each other, it was time to leave.

Chapter 4
Mistaken Identity

Maude grunted before spitting out her Skoal. Hippie watched her do so with both distaste and horror. How could anyone put that stuff into their mouths, chew on it like it were a big fat black gumball, and then spit it out with such gusto that the tobacco almost melted into the tar of the road? "Want some?" she asked, holding out the Skoal can as if she thought he'd consider the offer.

"No, thank you," he replied with as much courtesy as he could muster without throwing up. "I'll take another beer, though, if you're feeling charitable."

"Help yourself," she said, pushing the cooler across the picnic table with her beefy arms. She could beat him to a pulp if she wanted. Hippie was aware of that so didn't want to drink too much out of fear that he would say something that would offend her. Thus, he told himself that the can of Milwaukee's Best he pulled from the container would be his last for the day.

"How 'bout some beef jerky?" Maude asked. "It washes down with this beer real good."

"Okay," he found himself saying against every being in his nutrition-oriented mind. Were the four previous beers he had drunk starting to get to him? But this beer was mostly water. How could he be drunk already? Or was it that when his inhibitions were lowered, he actually liked unhealthy imitation crap, such as jerky?

He reached out and grabbed the already opened bag of jerky and scarfed down a piece. "Ummm, good!" he said, not lying. This was the first time he ate the stuff in many years. He did rather like the taste.

"It's my own recipe," Maude said proudly. "A dash of barbecue goes a long way." She took a piece and chomped it like she did the Skoal.

Oh, this is a woman of so much grace and eloquence! While his thoughts were sarcastic, he was fond of her straightforward crude manner.

They were sitting on a picnic table near the parking lot of the rest stop. Thus far, no one had bothered them, but Hippie noticed a few passersby briefly staring at them strangely. Why didn't people just mind their business? Why should they care if a long-bearded hippy and a bulky miscreant-looking woman chose to hang out together?

Just then, a pickup truck came to a halt on the grass near them. Two tattooed men were howling at the wind from the bed of the pickup as if they were threatening to turn into a werewolf. A third man, the driver, on the other hand, may have already been one. When he got out of the truck, Hippie could not tell if he had any skin on his arms, legs, or face underneath his hair. If not a werewolf, perhaps he was a bear.

"What do we have here?" one of the men asked after he finished howling. He leaped off the side of the truck.

"You got any of that jerky for us?" the second man said as he jumped off the tailgate.

"Don't you have some cat to chase?" Maude asked in reply, addressing both of them. "Or some cows to tip?"

"He haw," the first man said. "I think I may soon be tipping a cow. You're about as big as one."

"You better watch it, boy," Maude said, fists raised.

This was escalating out of control for Hippie's tastes, so he intervened. "We got plenty of jerky for everyone."

Maude turned and shushed him. "I got this," she added and raised her fists back up.

Meanwhile, the bear man had walked straight up to Hippie, seemingly just to stare at him. At first Hippie paid him no heed, focusing on what the others were up to, but soon this man's incessant staring became too annoying to ignore. "May I help you?" he asked.

"Are you Jesus?" Bearman questioned, seriously.

Normally one would think that to be a really odd question, but Hippie was used to it. In his travels, there had been many people who compared his appearance to Jesus or John Lennon or a younger Willie Nelson. However, by the sincerity in Bearman's voice and the fact that he looked like he was about to kneel and pray to him, this man was taking it to a whole new level. The fact that Hippie saw a gun underneath his jacket or fur (he wasn't sure which it was) made it more unusual, but Aspen wasn't worried about it. "Have you been watching too many repeats of *Duck Dynasty*?" he joked.

"What's that?" the man asked in reply.

Hippie was set aback by this. Who had ever heard of a redneck and a seemingly religious person to boot not knowing what *Duck Dynasty* was? "Oh, never mind, my disciple," he said with a smile.

Bearman looked confused and did not speak or make any movements, so Hippie took that opportunity to see how Maude was doing. He was just in time to witness Maude slapping around one of the goons as if he were from a three stooges' gag: a slap to the ear, a hit of the cheek, a pinch of his nose, and finally a punch to the chest. The punch sent the man staggering backwards until he tripped over the first goon whom Hippie now noticed was sprawled on the ground like a broken pretzel.

Maude wiped her hands together, her work done. She then stared in his direction. "Hey, Aspen, what's that guy doin'?" she asked, using his real name for effect.

He whirled around to see Bearman kneeling in prayer at his feet. "Now this is too much," Hippie said. "He really thinks I'm Jesus!"

"Has he even noticed that his friends are down and out?" Maude replied, still proud of her pugilistic accomplishments.

"Oh, my Lord, let me praise you in all your glory. You have returned to save us all!" Bearman continued his worship by attempting to kiss Hippie's feet, but he quickly moved away so that Bearman smooched grass instead.

"Maybe Jesus will come one day, but not right now. I'm not who you think I am," Hippie responded, and then added, "Get a grip!"

Bearman did get a grip—of Hippie's ankle! "I've touched God!" he proclaimed.

"Good God, stop this nonsense," Hippie said, trying to break free from the other's grip.

"Oh, I apologize," Bearman frantically yelled. "You are the son of God. I pray you forgive my mistake."

Hippie stopped struggling. This was useless. He would have to try a different tactic to escape this nut. "You are forgiven, my son." Then he added just for the fun of acting omnipotent, "As long as you are true to yourself and send love to all animals and plants alike. And you shall forever obey anyone who is truly a hippy of heart and spirit."

"I will heed your every word, Messiah."

"Be free then but leave me and be gone," Hippie decreed, stifling a chuckle.

Bearman released him and stood up, his worshipping finished. "Thank you, Jesus!"

And then he strode back to his pickup truck, started the ignition, and drove off. The two goons he came with still lay heaped on the ground, but he had not noticed and was unlikely to come back for them anytime soon, so enamored by seeing Jesus and all.

"Let's get back on the road," Maude said after Bearman's vehicle was out of sight. "Someone may come around and notice these clods soon." She stepped on one of those clods on her way to her truck, and he only whimpered in response.

Hippie followed Maude, bemused but happy at what had just happened to him. It wasn't every day that he got mistaken for being the almighty one, although it wasn't unprecedented.

He just had that appeal!

Chapter 5
A Glut of SUVs

Kenny couldn't be THAT drunk. Sure, Jade and Maria were keeping their distance as he punched the cushion seat next to him. Sure, it was kind of a weird thing to do because there was no real reason to hit taxi seats. Sure, he could have been doing something better with his time. But at least he realized what he was doing. He was just having fun. The cushion felt good against his fists.

In the middle of one of his punches, the cab suddenly stopped, throwing him under the passenger seat. Thus, his punch missed its mark, hitting the back of the front seat. George lurched forward, his seat belt tightened and cut against his neck. "Dammit, Kenny," George yelled. "I'm bleeding here."

Meanwhile, Bobarino screamed at a sign. "Detour, this city with its detours! How the hell am I supposed to get cross town this way?" Expletives erupted then, which Kenny could barely make out, his ears being caught between the passenger's seat and the backseat, which was hardly conducive to hearing.

"Get up, Kenny. You're crushing my legs," Jade said, adding to the commotion.

"I can't. I'm stuck," Kenny replied with his face jammed to the front seat, feeling mushed up like a bulldog.

"Get me a tissue," George said to no one.

"Stupid traffic," Bobarino complained.

"My legs!" Jade exclaimed.

"Mmmmmmm" was all Kenny could say as the cab lurched forward a couple of inches, forcing Kenny to kiss the passenger's seat.

"Help me, Maria," Jade commanded. Kenny had forgotten Maria was even in the cab. She had been silent this whole time. Maria did not respond but must have helped her friend because the next thing Kenny felt was the kick of Jade's sandal against his back as she pulled free.

"That hurts," Kenny whined.

"It serves you right," Jade responded.

"I still can't stop the bleeding," George complained.

"Screw you," Bobarino yelled at the neighboring SUV, which was honking uproariously for what seemed an hour. Bobarino returned the sentiment with his own honking. *That's New York City for you!*

With Jade's feet free, Kenny found room to free his face, but his butt was still wedged. "Please move your seat forward, Greg. I'm still stuck here."

"I'm bleeding because of you, so you'll just have to wait to free your drunk fat ass!" George's agitated voice demanded.

The taxicab skewed to the right, skirting the honking SUV as well as the other traffic. Looking up at the rearview mirror, Kenny saw Bobarino flash his middle finger back at the driver of the SUV. He also saw that the cab had pulled onto Thirtieth Street. "You're going the wrong direction," Kenny blurted out. "You're headed towards the Lincoln Tunnel."

Too late. Bobarino could not turn around before entering the tunnel. Thus, they were bound for New Jersey. *Ugh!*

On the bright side, Kenny's butt flew free when a tire slammed into a pothole just before entering the tunnel. Reacting to the bumps, however, he reflexively and accidentally kicked Maria's chin. At first, he was impressed with his kick, because the reach of his kick had been outstanding, but then he realized that Maria might be hurt.

"Oww! Watch it!" Maria screamed, her first words since Kenny entered this rollercoaster cab, but she looked uninjured.

"Still bleeding here!" George remarked.

"It's just a little scratch, you wimp," Jade announced back to George.

"Jersey! Damn detours!" Bobarino truly sounded disgusted.

Into the Lincoln Tunnel the cab zoomed, but keeping in one lane was difficult for Bobarino. He briefly swerved into the other lane, where he cut off another SUV with a Jersey license plate.

How ironic, Kenny thought. *Someone was cutting off a Jersey driver.* Kenny always seemed to see New Jersey drivers doing the cutting off.

However, the Jersey driver didn't even honk. What was going on here? Did the Lincoln Tunnel's lights make Jersey people react differently than usual?

Exiting the tunnel, Bobarino accidentally swerved again into the SUV's lane. This time, the other driver honked. And loudly at that. Indeed, it must have been the lights. Thus, for now, everything was back to normal.

Except that they were in New Jersey in the middle of the night in a cab driving ninety miles an hour. Bobarino certainly couldn't drive the speed limit. After all, he was a cab driver by profession.

Every cab driver always had something that made them stop the vehicle before it was necessary. A stop sign or a red light might do the trick, but Bobarino preferred to roll a stop sign and edge his way closer to a red light so that he would already be on the gas when the light turned green. Heavy traffic might work, but Bobarino would not stop unless there was absolutely nothing else to do. For instance, he had not completely stopped with the earlier Manhattan traffic and had entered the tunnel. Thus, the New Jersey Turnpike was looming.

What finally stopped this particular cab driver (but not necessarily a different one) was blowing a tire out due to a spike in the road. Before that eventuality, he had to swerve and then do a 360 before coming to a stop at the shoulder of the road inches from hitting a guard rail. At least the cab was no longer spinning out of control.

Even so, Kenny's stomach couldn't take the motion, and he vomited on Jade's sandals.

In return, Jade kicked him in the face, vomit flying onto his nose. "Jesus, Kenny, have respect for my shoes!"

Kenny did not react well, for the kicked vomit made him sneeze. The mucus from the sneeze reached Jade's other sandal.

"Disgusting!" Jade responded.

"I'm bleeding again," said George.

"That was fun!" announced Bobarino.

George got out of the cab, holding his cut neck like an infant might touch his mouth. The bleeding had clotted but George still seemed horrorstruck by the whole experience. Then, something else got his attention. "What's that stink?"

"Jersey!" all the others said at the same time.

"Enough," cried Maria as she opened the door and stepped out of the taxi. "What are we going to do now?" She finished her question right when another SUV sped past them, whipping dirt onto Maria's clothes. Unladylike, she flashed the SUV the middle finger.

"Beats me," Kenny yelled.

"Don't know," George admitted.

"Trashing my sandals, for one," Jade said, taking off her sandals and throwing them into the road.

Everyone looked at the highway and watched as a third SUV ran over one of the sandals. The shoe skidded down the highway along with the SUV like a ping-pong paddle smacking a ball on the ground. Fifty feet up, it broke away from the tire of the SUV and flew onto the shoulder of the highway.

"You do realize that you have nothing else to wear," Maria reminded Jade as they continued to watch the sandal spin like a top before finally coming to a halt. "And that you are standing on asphalt on the side of the New Jersey Turnpike on a relatively hot night."

If Jade hadn't realized the repercussions of what she had done immediately, she did so now. She hopped around as if she were walking on hot coal. Kenny guessed it wasn't far from the truth. She settled down when she jumped onto grass beside the road.

"Do you have a spare tire?" George asked Bobarino. "We usually have a donut in the trunk."

Bobarino shrugged, pulled the latch of the trunk, looked under the cushioning, and then shrugged again. "Guess not."

"Let's just call a tow truck," Maria said, always the rational one. She pulled out her phone. "What's your insurance's number?"

Bobarino shrugged again.

"You do have insurance?" Maria asked, incredulously.

Kenny expected Bobarino to shrug again and was not disappointed.

"George, call your father for the information," Maria said, taking control of the situation.

"He's not home. On a business trip. May be hard to reach. And it's late." George certainly appeared unwilling to call his dad, for he made no inclination to grab his phone from the cab. Kenny was not sure why since George's father, Paul, seemed friendly enough when he and Kenny had met.

"Then what do you propose we do?" Jade asked. This was the first time she talked directly to him since this whole crazy cab ride began.

George thought a moment. "Wait. Where are we?"

"Next to a highway," Bobarino said as he eyed the sandal that hadn't driven down the highway with the third SUV.

"In damn Jersey," Kenny said.

"Near Newark by the stink of things," added Maria.

"Secaucus, actually," Kenny replied, seeing a sign for MetLife Stadium, home to the Giants and Jets, although it was New Jersey (and not an insurance company). Beyond the sign, the traveling sandal settled.

"I know someone who lives around here. I met him playing his banjo in front of the book fair in Javitz. We've kept in touch since." A smile crossed George's face. He was excited by the prospect of visiting his friend.

"What kinda weirdo is he?" Jade asked, echoing Kenny's thoughts.

"Don't worry about it," George replied. "I'll just call him."

At that moment, a fourth SUV was honking at them, or more exactly, at Bobarino, who had ventured out onto the highway, presumably to retrieve the sandal. "Get off the highway!" the New Jersey SUV driver yelled out the window while swerving to avoid him.

Bobarino picked up the sandal and chucked it at the driver. Perhaps he had forgotten the reason he had gone to get it in the first place unless it simply was to toss it at any SUV passing by. The sandal slammed into the rear window, not breaking the glass but causing the driver of the SUV to screech to a stop right in the middle of the highway. Of course, a fifth SUV honked and yelled at the other driver before moving on.

Bobarino ran toward the stopped SUV in the highway, and other cars passed him on the left as if he were just an extraordinarily slow vehicle on the road. "What the hell were you doing, asshole?" the SUV driver asked, exiting his car and ready to fight.

"Yo, man, can't you see we need help over here?" replied Bobarino in his Italian, Greek, or an Eastern European accent (Kenny couldn't tell which).

The man in the SUV was built like a wiry Popeye on acid instead of spinach. He raised his muscled arms in a boxing stance. "We all fend for ourselves here in Jersey."

"Yeah, well us New Yorkers can knock out anyone in an SUV even if they are from Jersey," replied the cab driver. He nearly chuckled as he spoke and continued to advance toward the other man. The whole thing might have indeed been funny to Bobarino.

Kenny expected fists to fly as Acid Popeye went to meet him halfway. "You from the Bronx?" he asked.

"What's it to you? Are you a Yanks fan?" George had once told Kenny that Bobarino had beat up a man for talking trash about Derek Jeter before he retired. This whole affair might end up getting even uglier. Then, however, he realized one fact about north New Jersians: they ALL were Yankees fans to some degree.

"Yanks are pitching like shit, but they'll still win it all," said Acid Popeye. And just like that, the tension of the situation deflated.

"Yeah, they will," Bobarino said, now looking like he was going to hug the other man instead of killing him.

"Afraid I don't have a spare, buddy," Acid Popeye said, changing his tune and seeing why they were stranded. Can take you for help, though I don't know if we can find anything open at this time of night."

They walked to the cab, Acid Popeye's SUV still in the middle of the highway with no hazard lights on. George approached them, talking excitedly. "Can you take us to Main Street in Secaucus? I know someone who lives there. He'll be able to help."

"Sure thing, buddy." Kenny guessed that Acid Popeye thought of all of them as buddies now.

They all walked toward the SUV. Bobarino looked back. "What about the cab? We're near Newark. It could be stripped or something."

"Well, unless you want to stay by the cab until we get back, there's not much we can do," Kenny said, finally beginning to sober up. The punching cushion session was finally out of his system.

Bobarino contemplated, and then continued to the SUV. All five passengers fit in the large vehicle without an issue, but Kenny was thankful that Acid Popeye had been the only one in the car beforehand.

They were off. The driver seemed to know his way around the area, and George helped him find the building where his friend lived. Kenny wondered who this friend was, for he had not heard George mention this person, nor had he known that George liked to read. Why else would he have been at Javitz during a book fair?

He hoped everything would work out, but his sobered thoughts told him otherwise. Kenny had a feeling that the craziness had only just begun.

Chapter 6
The Chase and the Capture

Outside, Freckles looked around the great wilderness. When Yellowstone Park was your backyard, even a Rottweiler used to the country had to admire the expansive milieu. But he could explore later. Right now, he had important business to attend to. He took his dump on the road.

When he finished, he admired his handiwork. A park ranger or some pedestrian would find that one, for sure. Sometimes he had to make his presence known. After all, what other dogs in the area could dump something that beautiful?

Turning aside from his handiwork, Freckles spotted a rodent sprint by him. By the smell of it, he quickly determined it to be a chipmunk. He considered chasing it but dismissed the notion when he smelled the scent of a different animal, one he was sure he had never encountered. Curious, he followed his nose.

When close, he looked up to see a small animal race past him. Indeed, he had never seen the likes of it before. Sure, it sort of looked like a squirrel with its bushy tail, but it was not any kind of squirrel he had seen. And by the looks of things, this animal was chasing the chipmunk. Who had ever heard of a squirrel chasing a chipmunk?

In any case, Freckles knew that he had to get a move on it if he were to witness any more of the chase. He ran after them, a dog on an escapade.

In the dusk, Freckles had to rely on his nose and ears more than usual. He was often a visual dog, as many a Rottweiler can be, hence the reason they are good watchdogs, but he was still a dog, and smell was his focal sense. Thus, he believed that he could follow the chipmunk and the other animal easily enough.

But the animals raced towards the woods and through the bushes where Freckles had more and more trouble navigating. Those Jack Russell digger dogs might have already caught up with the animals he was chasing, but his Rottweiler frame was just too large to maneuver around bushes and bramble. He would just have to plow through, not worrying about thorns or poison ivy.

These little hassles wouldn't disturb his fun. He thrashed through the thicket like a Doberman might do when suddenly free from his tethering. The chipmunk and the odd other rodent now certainly sensed the trouble they could be in.

Of course, Freckles would not hurt them, though. He was in it only for the fun of the chase.

The thrashing through the woods seemed to work. He was catching them, although the trailing unnamed animal gave him no heed.

Then the chipmunk simply disappeared. How could this be? Freckles still smelled the rodent. And quite close by too.

The other animal clued him back in by beginning to burrow into what once was an excavated rabbit's den. This gave Freckles time to catch up, but still the weird animal did not pay him any attention.

The big dog recklessly bounded toward his quarry with joy and gusto. When he made it to within a few paces, the bushy tailed multi-brown-colored animal whirled around—teeth snarling and claws extended, ready to strike.

Did this animal think he stood a chance against a Rottweiler? Freckles grinned in merriment, but he did not advance any closer. He had no reason to. He did not wish to harm this creature.

The chipmunk took that moment to ditch its hiding place and attempt its escape. The multi-brown-colored animal with ears like a fox saw this and leapt after the chipmunk.

For Freckles, that meant the chase would continue. He barked with glee.

The dog ran and ran. Nothing could stop him when he was on the chase. He scrunched sticks, jumped rocks, sloshed through mud, and continued to thrash bushes. However, somehow the rodents kept ahead of him. That was until they reached the tallest fir tree in the area. Freckles recognized it because he had been this way before. It was the great Douglas-fir tree, which he nicknamed Grand Fetcher. Whenever he visited, he retrieved branches, or he chewed on bones. The branches and cones obviously fell from the tree, but where the bones came from and from which small animals were mysteries to him.

The chipmunk attempted to lose the other animal in the substantial growth of the tree, but the other creature navigated the inner branches with ease. It could not be stopped easily. And that thing was hungry!

Then the chipmunk did something Freckles had never seen a chipmunk do: it climbed up the tree. This was a normal practice for squirrels, but chipmunks were ground critters.

But the other animal could climb trees too, and Freckles began to realize that the chipmunk would not escape without help. Normally, the chase would end without any harm being done to the other animals, and Freckles liked the chipmunk's tenacity, so he decided that he would help it escape. This other animal would find other pickings on this night anyway, Freckles was sure.

The dog leapt into Grand Fetcher as if it were a broken fence, right below where the animals were climbing. The predator animal had not expected anything to come blasting below him, so it lost its grip on the branch and fell to the ground, unhurt. This gave the chipmunk its chance to escape.

But Freckles was now entangled by the branches. He had to be careful to escape being scratched or suffering worse injuries. He was caught in such a way that his paws could not reach the ground. Perhaps he had been a little too quick to jump into the fir tree, but he had saved the chipmunk. That made him grin.

As he wiggled his torso and stepped gingerly through the limbs with each paw, he saw that the strange animal was glaring at him, scrutinizing his every move and remembering exactly what he looked like. Freckles made a note to find out what this creature was so that he could deal with it better if he were to see it again.

Then Freckles stepped on a branch and gave off the most innocent of yelps. The yelp was not much of anything, but the rodent, or whatever it was, heard him. It grinned with its undersized mouth and snickered. Was it laughing it him? This creature had nerve!

In any case, the unrestricted animal took that moment to disappear in the brush, and Freckles could not chase it because of his current predicament. He hoped this was not the only time he met this snickering, ears-like-a-fox, multi-brown-colored, bushy-tailed creature, for he now had a score to settle.

Back to the problem at hand, Freckles attempted to reach down with his paw in an attempt to touch ground. He stretched but not quite far enough. The limbs seemed to have him like a rope or a strangulated snake, so he wiggled some more—

And saw the tail of a real snake on him! Was this where the snake always lay in wait for prey? Was the snake attempting to strangle his body? Is that why Freckles found so many bones here? He wiggled violently this time, and the snake flew off him like a bird without wings.

Then he saw what type of snake it was and grinned again. A Rubber Boa, the smallest snake in the boa family. At a wimpy two feet long, that snake couldn't wrap itself around Freckle's torso. A boa constrictor it wasn't. The rubber boa hadn't bitten him either. Maybe it had just come onto the scene to see what all the hubbub was about? Freckles gave the snake the benefit of the doubt.

But now what to do? He was still no closer to escaping the tree. He tried to bite at the branches without success. He attempted to wiggle and worm his way free, but something still would not release him. Finally, thinking of nothing else, he barked. He was not a fan of barking, unlike many of his breed, but sometimes you just had to bring attention to yourself. Barking was also fun while on a chase.

No one came for him, of course. He was too far from anyone who could help. A hummingbird heard his bark but just hummed by him; it couldn't help.

Freckles continued to wiggle and worm and bite and claw, and yes, bark, but all that got him was more stuck. It seemed that he had landed between branches that entangled him more when he struggled. Worse, night was almost here now. Well, at least he wasn't hurt or even that uncomfortable. Perhaps he could just rest a little before trying to escape again.

He must have drifted off because he dreamed of many hummingbirds coming to his rescue. They flew through the branches, opening some space between the branches as others pecked at them. Then they hummed off, back to their own pursuits. But in the dream, he was free.

And he fell to the ground, waking. He was freed, but there were no hummingbirds nearby. How'd he escape? Had he freed himself in his sleep? Or had he not really been asleep, and his dream had not been a dream at all? Had hummingbirds actually freed him? He might never know for sure.

What Freckles did realize was that he was making friends and enemies. He raced home, thinking of ways to thank the hummingbirds, no matter if they had really helped or not. But also, he relished the chance to get back at the dastardly creature whose species' name he did not yet know.

Chapter 7
Waterskiing 101

According to Hippie and many others of his persuasion, niacin is the most pleasurable of vitamins. Sure, it may make you turn red for a while and you may itch, but it flushes out the system. Hippie took the pain so that he could be healthy. Whenever he felt anxious or out of sorts he just popped a B-3 pill, and in a half hour or so he was feeling good. That's if he hadn't drunk any alcohol in a while, for niacin and alcohol didn't mix well for him. *This ain't no detox; it's a cleansing. Let's put those capillaries to work so that the blood rids itself of toxins!*

So after falling asleep in Maude's truck for the night and not feeling any ill effects of Milwaukee's Best, he popped a pill of Niacin. He would take two if necessary but no more. Too much was not good. He'd found out the hard way one time after taking a third pill, which had made him feel itchy for hours and red for what seemed like days.

Hippie stepped out and began his ritualistic walk around the truck stop. After a dozen or so steps, he began his dance, as if he were calling the sky to rain. Instead, though, his face turned bright red, and the dancing became more of an itching frenzy. Maude returned from the outhouse and saw him in motion. "Hey, look, Raggedy Ann is dancing like it's 1999! Let's Go Crazy and bring the Raspberry Beret!" Hippie was aware of Maude's obsession with Prince's music. She played his music constantly throughout their trip together, although she never played anything from his "Symbol" period of music. That was sacrilegious! *Especially after his death. RIP, Prince.*

Hippie did not reply. He was too busy dancing out the itches as quickly as he could. While he rather liked feeling hot and itchy, he enjoyed the aftereffects much more. Thus, he danced chaotically, not caring about any embarrassment. Why should he care what other people thought of him or his actions? People tended to think fondly of him anyway.

He danced on.

"Are you doing the chicken dance?" Maude continued, "Or is the red beak you're sporting for sheer entertainment?"

Hippie couldn't help but scratch his blush nose, for the niacin itched him silly. He continued to dance because it was helping the discomfort move along or at least stopped him from thinking about it too much.

Maude began to slap her knee and kick her legs as if she were at some hoedown, but she had a completely different rhythm than he did. He just moved any which way that felt good. "Let's play some redneck country music now, 'cause you're redder than anyone I've seen, and the sun isn't even out strong this morn."

She must have temporarily run out of material because she left then. Hippie guessed she was done ragging on him for the moment. He was glad of it since he had to concentrate on nothing but flushing out his system. He felt his blood course through him as clean as untouched arctic water, and he was beginning to cool off. A hematic chill seeped through him, and he felt healed of mind and body.

Maude's truck pulled up. Blaring from the speakers was a country song that could have been played at a square-dance shindig. "Yep, this seems like a good accompaniment to your chicken dance."

He slowed his dance because the itching and redness were subsiding. Soon, only his natural cleanse would remain.

"Are you done there yet? I want to be in Lake Tahoe by the end of the morn. Have friends there waiting for me after I deliver my packages. Got you a sesame seed bagel with some egg whites. That's the kind of shit you like when you're not eating jerky, right?"

He stopped dancing then. "Not really. Bagels aren't any good for you, and eating a real egg would be just fine with me," Hippie said. "But thank you for thinking of me."

All the way to Lake Tahoe, the niacin felt pure coursing through his system. The goodness flowed through his capillaries, reaching every nook and cranny of his body, from his ears all the way to his pinky toe. He enjoyed the feeling but knew it wouldn't last. He would have to eat and drink something other than pure water soon. The food would then release toxins into his body, ending his healthy ecstasy. After a bit more reveling in his wholesome state, he grabbed the bagel and egg whites and chomped into them. The bagel was a bit hard because of the hours it had sat, but it did sate his hunger.

He felt fine, though. He would take more niacin only when he believed the time to be right, if only to revel in it more. He knew that it was better to take it in moderation.

"There's Lake Tahoe," Maude said as if he were a dolt who could not see the lake right in front of him. "What's your plan now?"

"I thought I might take in some waterskiing," he said.

Maude laughed, not realizing that Hippie was serious. "Here, you might need these." She handed him a pair of plastic gloves. "Might protect you from your hands getting chapped."

"Oh, thanks," Hippie said, taking the gloves.

Maude looked chagrined. She had offered him the gloves in jest. "Umm, I have to make my delivery. Where should I drop you off?"

Ignoring the question, Hippie asked, "Oh, what are you delivering?" This was the first time he had asked. What she delivered was her business, not his, but curiosity had finally edged its way forward.

"Plants, logs, glass, and minerals," she replied.

"But there are plenty of those here."

"Not the type I have."

This piqued his curiosity, an occurrence that rarely happened. "How so?"

"Well, I sell petrified logs and precious minerals, amongst other stuff," replied Maude. "And that's all you need to know right now."

Were these items stolen? Or were they illegal in some other way, such as being produced in an unlawful factory or taken from a protected natural resource location? Were the minerals some sort of new trafficked drug on the market? Was Maude being paid a large sum of money to get these items into the wrong hands? Whatever the case, Hippie let it be.

"Okay, drop me off at the ski boat rental place. I have to get my water sport on." And with that, he forgot about the items in the back of the truck.

"You really going?"

"Damn straight, I am," he replied, automatically entering Aspen mode as if he had just flicked a switch in himself. As a teen, before he

Adam Altman

became the hippy he was, Aspen had a phase wherein he tried all types of water sports, from Marco Polo to surfing, from water volleyball to synchronized swimming, from tubing to waterskiing. Aspen tried them all, and sometimes he still had a hankering to do one or more of them.

They pulled up to the rental place. The first person he saw was a long-haired blonde, blue-eyed lad with a waterproof necklace around his neck, who was carrying a surfboard under his arm. The surfer was so stereotypical looking that he could see him "acting" in a lame-brained B movie, where the surfer saves the world and gets the girl.

"Have a blast," said Maude. "Be back around later. If you're still here, maybe I'll have some beef jerky for ya."

"Thank you. That would be great!" Hippie exclaimed as he departed the truck while waving goodbye.

Aspen (no longer thinking himself to be Hippie till his sporting activities finished) didn't go to the rental counter. Instead, he waited outside for someone to walk out. "Hey, dude," said the surfer boy. "You ready for the water?"

"You know that this is Lake Tahoe, not an ocean. I doubt you'll be seeing many waves," replied Aspen as politely as could be.

"Dude, I know that. Just came back from the coast. Bringing the board to my truck and then will be renting out a boat with my buds." He pointed to the group of people just exiting the rental place. "You with us?"

And just like that, he joined their group.

The boaters were a ragtag team. Aspen and the blonde surfer-dude, named Joe, were accompanied by a young cook who slaved over a pizza oven at night and was the captain of the rental boat by day; a long-haired thirty-something woman who looked much older due to being out in the California sun for most of her life; a pothead drifter; and a teenaged boy, who happened to be Joe's younger brother. All of them welcomed Aspen as if he had always been one of the gang.

As it turned out, the sun-soaked woman was an advanced water skier. "How is your technique?" she asked Aspen when they were out on the lake.

"Don't have any technique. I just go where the boat and the ripples lead me." That was his way, whether he was sporting Aspen or fun-loving Hippie. He just went with the flow. He didn't possess any formal training in anything. While he did graduate high school, had taken a few college classes, and had an acuity to learn, he never stayed at anything long enough to acquire an actual trade or talent, although he was good at most things.

"Well, let's see how you do it. Are you ready?" she asked with her gray eyes open wide. Had the sun drained all the color from her eyes?

"I'm game," he said. He was nearly always game.

Before long, Aspen found himself on the skis, ready to rock. The drifter had decided to play an album from the band, Van Halen, which came out when Sammy Hagar was the lead singer. "Standing on Top of the World" blared from his small box. This pothead, for a fatty rested between the drifter's fingers, probably hadn't even heard of an iPod. Oddly, the others of the group never asked him for a hit.

Standing on top of the skis, Aspen was ready. When the boat set off, Aspen was less ready. When the boat sped up, Aspen was ready for trouble. When the boat reached full speed, Aspen readied himself for a tumble.

Before the tumble, however, a duck quacked into view. He skirted the mallard but lost his balance as the boat tugged forward. His skis flipped over, and for one solid second he flew through the air with only the tip of the skis touching the water, like Aquaman if he could fly. Aspen reached forward with his poles still in his hands, facing forward, and dived into the water. The skis slammed the surface of the water after he was completely underwater and then snapped off his feet. Meanwhile, he zipped to the lake floor, poles sticking into rock and slime. Aspen released the poles only after his momentum had reversed. He surfaced before having the inclination to start swimming.

"That was epic," said Joe when he saw him.

"Totally rad," added his brother.

"Couldn't have done that even if I were Aquaman," the captain cheered.

"Quite lucky you're not hurt," the sun-soaked woman said, telling it like it was.

And the man with the joint stared into space, apparently missing the entire sequence.

Treading water, Aspen spoke apologetically. "I'll go swim down the equipment, don't you worry," he said to the woman. "I guess I need those lessons, huh?"

"Damn straight," said the woman. Until then, Aspen had thought he was the only one who still spoke that idiom.

For the next fifteen minutes, Aspen retrieved the skis and poles, diving here and fro to find the poles and swimming with the trifling current until he finally gathered the skis. Neither had been damaged. The skis had come off his feet but had not snapped as he had originally thought. After a bit of doing, he was able to uncork the poles from the bottom of the lake.

"That was fun! Got my heart rate up more than the actual waterskiing."

"You got to clean up your own mess, Aspen. That's one of my rules of the boat," the captain decreed.

"He has many rules," said Joe.

"Many, many rules," his brother added.

"Too many rules," said the sun-soaked woman.

The drifter just stared at the sky.

Aspen heard many of those rules during the next few hours while he was boating with them. Some made sense, such as rule number one: "Don't fall off the boat, especially when sharks infest the waters or where sharp rocks can impale you." Some made partial sense, such as rule number forty-two: "The sail is your friend, unless there's wind at your mast in the rain." And some were just inane, such as rule number eighty-three: "The soda bottles on my boat love me."

The woman of the boat gave Aspen some pointers on waterskiing, but he only went out on the skis one more time, skiing without incident until the boat came to a standstill. Even though he had learned about stopping from past lessons and from a few of the woman's pointers, he still didn't get it right. He skied into the boat and keeled over its side. He wasn't injured, but the incident did prompt the captain's rule number fifty-six: "Too much upheaval could lead to ruin." Aspen thought this one made some kind of sense but seemed also to be inane. As the numbers got higher, the more ridiculous the rules seemed to get.

Perhaps there was a reason for the captain to number them the way he did, but Aspen doubted it.

'Are you having a good time?" Joe asked at one point near the end of the day.

"I always do," replied Aspen, but in truth he was beginning to miss his Hippie self. Aspen could only come out to play for so long. Not that he was schizophrenic, for he knew full well when he wanted to partake in Sporting Aspen activities. That's why he had come waterskiing in the first place.

"Time to dock," the captain said, as if no one else knew what was happening. Even the smoking drifter seemed to notice that the boat was docking—in-between his empty gazes and his munching on M&Ms.

Joe slapped Hippie's shoulder (for Aspen had finished his fun). "Why don't you come with us again one of these days? You're a fun guy, and we welcome that."

Hippie was used to these invitations and always accepted them gratuitously. "Yes, we may meet again for boating or whatever comes our way." And Hippie believed this because he did seem to run into the same people again and again, although it could be days, months, or years between visits.

However, this visit with this particular group was about to come to an end, for as soon as they returned to the boat rental place, Maude pulled up in her truck. "We gotta be going," Maude spoke hurriedly through the window and opened the passenger's side door for him. Anxiety was apparent in her brutish face.

He got in without much thought. If he had been thinking, he would have realized that he wasn't involved in the trouble that Maude had likely gotten into, that he had no reason to go with her, and that he was hungry; Maude had no food, not even jerky, in the truck. And if he had stayed in Lake Tahoe longer, he could have avoided everything that was about to happen. But Hippie always seemed to find himself in interesting situations. So why should this be any different?

Maude peeled out with Hippie in tow. Where they were going now, he couldn't guess. He knew, however, that he'd be in Wyoming eventually.

He always ended up there.

Chapter 8
Faulkner

George Cramwell had not always been the standup guy he was today. As a mischievous youth, he had gone astray on a number of occasions. In elementary school, he had vandalized a mosque, not knowing that it was a Muslim place of worship. In the middle of the night, he and a couple of "friends" had broken a window to get in even though the front door was open. Then, he sprayed paint all over the floor. He had meant to paint a cute dog on a dare from one of those so-called friends, but his artistry lacked talent and the painting looked nothing like a cuddly dog. Instead of the whole thing being a cute joke as he had intended, the imam of the mosque had been offended because he thought the graffiti represented a symbol against Muslims, although George still did not know what the imam thought had been drawn. Of course, art or no art, offensive or not, what he did was still vandalism. There was a lot of hoopla about what had happened until no more acts against the mosque quieted things down. And he hadn't got caught. While he didn't vandalize the mosque again, his crime spree was just beginning.

He was such an impressionable youth that he copied what his "friends" did, so one day he robbed a convenience store just for a few packs of gum, some Combos, and a crisp one-dollar bill. He did it for the thrill and from the insistence of the riffraff he hung out with. On many occasions, he did small acts of theft, from stealing a Walkman from his father's friend's house to taking fireworks from fellow kids.

His vandalism didn't stop either, and the need to do it again increased each time he didn't get caught, but his luck finally ran out. When vandalizing the playground of his childhood elementary school for no other reason than because he felt like it, a custodian spotted him, so he ran. To escape, he jumped a fence, but his pants got caught on the wire coils at the top of the fence and ripped. His favorite pants had been ruined, and that marked him. Thus, because of this travesty with his pants, the impressionable sixteen-year-old had stopped his crime spree. In retrospect, however, what happened right after that was what truly changed his life forever. In his haste to escape, he had run the back trails and smashed right into a teen by the name of Aspen Mitchell, who he came to know later as Hippie.

At first, George was startled by bumping into the unkempt young man, who was smoking something or other in the middle of the woods. George suspected marijuana, but the substance didn't smell anything like it, and if it were some strange variance of it, it was a pleasant one. Upon closer inspection, George saw that the young man was not smoking at all. He was chewing on eucalyptus leaves.

"You seem to have lost your way," Hippie had told him.

"I'm not sure I ever knew the way," George replied, thinking about how his escape had led him to these woods.

"Apropos," replied Hippie. George had just run into him but was immediately impressed by the young man's demeanor and atypical sophistication. Although he looked rugged, there was a sort of quality to him that made him both friendly and wise for his years.

"What brought you here?" George asked.

"Nature and tranquility. You should try it some time." Hippie took another chew before spitting out a few of the eucalyptus leaves from his mouth. "Tranquility beats acting out any day of the week." That's all Hippie said on the subject, but George took it to heart nevertheless. The next time he thought about committing a petty act of graffiti, he found himself wandering into nature instead, and later, he took up paint and brush on canvas instead of on someone's wall.

"Why are you eating those leaves?"

"Cures the cold, my friend," but Hippie spit the rest of the eucalyptus leaves away. "Too much of it, though, can be poisonous," he continued. "I think I've chewed just enough to feel its homeopathic effect. No sense in taking any chances with it when I'm feeling good."

George found himself wanting to discover more of what Hippie had to say. Eventually, he would find out that seeking Hippie's advice was a common occurrence. There was just something about him, unexplainable but there nevertheless. "Where did you learn about these leaves?"

"16 ½ Street," Hippie replied as if he were saying, "Main Street," but then writing the mixed number in the dirt.

"Where's that?" George asked.

"California," Hippie answered and then began to talk about his friend Faulkner.

Thus, a dozen-plus years ago, George first found out about the street that would lead him to the man they were now visiting on Main Street in Secaucus, New Jersey.

Now, when you first encountered someone on 16 ½ Street, that person would not be considered normal in society. Since George had only visited, he could still pass in society, but Faulkner had a lot more trouble with normalcy because he grew up on 16 ½ Street somewhere in a tiny town in Central Valley. At fifty-two years of age, living on 16 ½ Street for forty of them and in New Jersey for the other twelve, Faulkner believed that the world revolved around Joshua trees, Camaros, and the sun. For a person who lived in the two places he had, at least he cared about the sun, and therefore, the environment by association.

Though his name would suggest otherwise, Faulkner wasn't much into literary pursuits. As a matter of fact, he was not one to read much at all, for picture books seemed to be his limit. In this way, he fit in perfectly with Jersey culture.

However, when George and his friends walked into his apartment, many copies of William Faulkner's *The Sound and the Fury* were enshrined in his small cluttered apartment. So, it seemed that the person he was named after had influenced his life after all, but George still doubted that his friend had read the masterpiece. After all, the man also displayed a rather large Joshua tree in the middle of his living space with toy Camaros encircling it, like a new dimensional solar system that could only be seen in Jersey or the desert parts of California.

"Welcome, my friend," Faulkner greeted. "Long time no see. When did we meet last?"

"Saw you in Jersey City once last year. You were selling things on the street and singing folk songs with your banjo." George remembered that day with fondness. Not only had he heard him play a jamming rendition of "Foggy Mountain Breakdown," he had also bought a cool Matchbox car from him, one he hadn't seen since he was a kid.

"Oh, yeah. Still play there on occasion, although people there no longer know good music when they hear it." Maybe that was the case, but it didn't help that Faulkner looked scruffier than ever with a half chopped-off beard and dirt on his nose. Oddly, however, he didn't smell all that bad.

Meanwhile, Bobarino switched off his cell phone. "Looks like we're here for the night. A tow truck can't get to the cab until the morn."

"Welcome to stay," said Faulkner, always willing to lend a hand. "Be crowded. Most of you hafta sleep on the floor. My bed is big enough for two though," and he gave a seemingly lewd look toward Maria.

Maria stepped up, ready to sock him when Faulkner added, "George and Jade can take my bed. I'm sort of used to the floor anyway. Maria can take the couch." George noticed Maria relax then, no longer sure what to think. Faulkner might seem lewd, but George remembered him as a more of a eunuch than a hound dog.

"We're no longer together," Jade said quickly. "Not that you should have known that we were together in the first place."

"All right then. Just figure out the sleepin' arrangements amongst yourselves. If you want anything to drink, there's beer and water in the fridge." Faulkner picked up a copy of *The Sound and the Fury* and began thumbing through it. It seemed that he had had enough of the current conversation.

"You read the book?" George asked.

"Yeah, a bunch a times. Only novel I ever read."

"I heard that book is kind of difficult to read." George knew nothing about the book except that this was a common opinion of it.

"Na, what do you mean? It's only four chapters about brothers obsessing over this girl, Caddy."

"You know, Faulkner, that Caddy's their sister," chimed in Maria, who evidently knew more than George did.

"Of course. You think I stupid or something," Faulkner replied, speaking grammar wrongly. On purpose or not, George could not be sure. He did tend to talk with some bad grammar, but this one could have been intentional.

"If I can play the banjo, I can understand my own work," Faulkner finished.

"You mean the book you read, right?" Maria inquired.

"Yeah, read it and wrote it. My name is on the cover, don't you see?"

Maria looked at George, silently asking, "Is he serious?" George just shrugged.

Faulkner handed the book to Kenny, who seemed to still be recovering from all the alcohol he had drunk so had not yet uttered a word in the apartment. He looked at the book and saw Faulkner on the cover, but the name William was nowhere to be found. Subsequently he unfolded it, for it was not a book at all. Instead, what now lay outspread was a poster annotating the song, "The Sound and the Fury."

George laughed. "I knew you couldn't read the William Faulkner book, but I bet the song is good."

"It will be a banjo classic. Mark my words. Right up there with "Cotton-Eyed Joe" and "Doggy Salt," remarked Faulkner, eying his apartment, apparently looking for his banjo.

George nodded his agreement, keeping silent about the fact that he had never heard of the song, "Doggy Salt." "Let's have a listen," he said, seeing that his friends immediately frowned at his suggestion. Bobarino even went as far as to leave the room, supposedly because he needed to go to the bathroom.

But his friends had never heard Faulkner play. The man might be a lot of things, but he was also a fantastic banjo player.

That excellent musician wasn't one for tidiness. The apartment was so cluttered that George could not see most of the carpet. No wonder Faulkner was having trouble spotting his banjo.

The banjo might not be in the room either, for Faulkner was notorious for leaving his banjo in weird places. As a matter of fact, he had planned to leave 16 1/2 Street a month earlier than he had, but it had taken him that long to find his banjo, which had somehow ended up in a hammock atop a tree. George had never found out how it had gotten there or how it had survived the weather that entire time. He was not certain if Faulkner knew, either.

Jade stepped into Faulkner's view before he could locate the banjo, if it was indeed in the living room. "Get me some clean sheets and Maria and I will take your bed." Yep, there it was again: Jade in command mode. Why did he like her so much?

Faulkner looked perplexed as he searched around the room. Evidently, both his banjo and clean sheets were difficult to locate. After a moment, he decided that it would be best if he looked elsewhere, so he walked to his bedroom.

The host was gone for quite a while, so the men picked areas of the floor that appeared most sanitary on which to sleep, leaving the couch for Faulkner. After all, he had been gracious enough to welcome them this late at night. Whether the accommodations were comfy or not mattered little to George, at least for only a few hours, although he knew that Jade would disagree.

"I found a clean blanket and a top sheet," Faulkner announced excitedly, sheet in hand. "You ladies can do without a fitted sheet, right?"

Before Jade could answer negatively, Maria spoke out. "They'll do."

The women went into the bedroom as Faulkner realized that the couch had been left for him and sat on it. Immediately, George heard a twang and a crunch, like a country song gone bad, and the musician jumped up. "Found my banjo. Under the couch cushion the whole time."

Faulkner's weight had crushed the banjo. "Can you still play it?" George asked.

"Break it all the time. I'll have it fixed by the morning." With those words, Faulkner took the banjo and opened a door that George had not noticed. Faulkner walked through and did not come out until morning.

After a few moments, Bobarino couldn't wait any longer and took the couch as his resting place. George scrunched in the corner next to a real copy of *The Sound and the Fury* and used the book as his pillow.

George fully expected to be tossing and turning against the wall and bumping his head against the book all night, but instead, he went out like a log and found comfort in the pages of the book. Perhaps that was a sign that he should read more. He told himself he would try to read a William Faulkner book (not the Faulkner song) when he was back home, relaxed in his apartment.

In the morning with banjo fixed, Faulkner began to play and sing in a low, melodic, yet jumpy voice:

In Jefferson, the Sound and the Fury awakens my wraith;
Dying, dying, dying townsmen.
A systematic thirty years of family gone down a path
Where finances die of way back when...

"Tell me the truth," George interrupted. "Did you actually read the entire book or just the back cover?"

"Of course, as I said yesterday, I read the whole book. Many times," Faulkner responded, unoffended by any hint that George might have given to Faulkner's past illiteracy. "I needed inspiration for the song." *Okay, there is that.* Although after he thought about it later, the song had nothing to do with the book and had been composed long before Faulkner had the education to fully read and understand it. Nonetheless, Faulkner's own inane comprehension of the novel had led to the song. George left it at that, now coming to believe his friend.

Stopping his song, Faulkner simply said, "Time to go," and they all packed into his old beat-up Datsun and drove to where the cab lay. The roadside assistance vehicle was already there. The only problem was that most of the cab wasn't. The tires, including the flat, had been stripped, the windshield whippers taken, the trunk jacked, the doors fully opened with the radio, cushions, and steering wheel gone. "No engine either," said the roadside assistance driver when he looked under the hood of the cab. "Still just want a new tire?" he continued, facetiously.

They were shit out of luck. When they had left, George had had a nagging suspicion that something like this would happen. After all, they were too close to Newark. What could they do now?

Damn Jersey!

Chapter 9
This One's for the Birds

"That damned weasel or whatever it is has been stirring up trouble again," said Harrison one morning from the porch deck. Freckles perked up his ears.

"It's a pine marten, Harry. I've told you that many times," Lana yelled back to him from somewhere on the other side of the house. Freckles heard her and now had the name of that dastardly creature. Finally!

"Took our berries right from the high bush. We barely have any blueberries left. Thought at that height that critter wouldn't get to them," Harrison continued, staring right at the bush, but the marten was not there. Freckles would have charged right through the screen door if it had been shut. That creature had to be taught a lesson.

"They can climb bushes, you know." Lana walked into the kitchen and patted Freckles on the head. He liked that. It made him feel comfy, as his hair puffed up, giving him a cool chill. This time, however, Lana stopped patting him before that effect could be achieved.

"Don't those things mostly eat mice? Why our blueberries?"

"I don't know, dear." Freckles thought about the chase. It seemed that this one preferred chipmunks and blueberries over mice.

"Well, enough is enough. I'm going to set a trap for it," Harrison said. Freckles' ears perked up again. Then he barked softly with excitement.

"No, you're not," replied Lana, who always stopped everything Harrison wanted to do, which was usually the correct action. "You'll get yourself or someone else hurt or will kill that innocent creature."

Innocent? Hardly! Freckles still had a few scratches from when he had first met the marten.

"I'm handy. I can do this," Harrison spoke assuredly.

Freckles watched as Lana did something with her eyes. She did that often when Harrison spoke about something she didn't think was true.

"Stop rolling your eyes," Harrison confirmed.

"You can't even see me."

"I know you, though." With that, Harrison walked off to the tool shed, not giving his wife a chance to dismiss his idea.

Freckles wanted to go with him. There must be something in the shed that he could paw if the marten showed up. "Woof," he barked, only to get Lana's attention, and lightly scratched the back-glass door.

"You want to check up on my fool of a husband, boy," Lana said. "Are you going to protect him from his follies?"

"Woof," Freckles responded with his most good-intentioned bark.

"Don't you go knocking over anything like you did last summer, Freckles." His female caretaker always brought that up whenever he went to the shed. He hadn't known the rake was there, so he couldn't help but step on it, which lifted the handle up and knocked into other tools. This caused a chain reaction of tools falling and the work bench breaking. Freckles had narrowly escaped a flying screwdriver to the ear. He had heard it whiz by him like an angry wasp. The sound still haunted him.

"Woof," he replied, acknowledging his past mistakes and promising not to do so again with his concise bark.

"Okay then," said Lana, sliding the door open for him. Freckles ran out, looked back at Lana for one quick grin, and took off for the shed.

Harrison was already there, sorting through junk, which was most of the shed's contents. He went through cardboard boxes and newspapers, like they were old news, but he mostly fidgeted with cracked bicycles, which had been ridden when Harrison was a lad — five dog generations ago. That bike had not been ridden since Rags was a pup. Freckles had heard about Rags, the Saint Bernard from numerous Harrison youthful stories. As a matter of fact, it may have been Rags who wrecked the bike.

"What do you think, Frecks? What can make a good trap for that rascal of a marten? I was thinking of using this brake pedal so that it could be knocked out at just the right angle. Then the basket would trap it. The weasel could be baited with the blueberries."

Freckles nuzzled against Harrison's leg, giving him encouragement, although the Rottweiler was uncertain that something that simple would capture that smart-alecky marten.

Ridicula

"Did I ever tell you about the time me and Rags chased down that rattler that spooked a little boy? We wanted to make the rattler see how scared it could be. And as big a dog as Rags was, the rattler was plenty scared. Rags was smart enough to keep out of striking distance but swiped at the snake before it could bite. Rags threw the snake clear across the road. Not sure if it survived." Freckles recognized the smile of when Harrison reminisced. His face was gleaming now.

His longish "woof" was always Freckle's reply to any given story. He had heard this one many times before, but that didn't matter. His "woof" was still apropos.

"We might have a similar adventure with this weasel creature, Frecks," continued Harrison. "We'll have some fun."

Freckles knew that the man might be in for more than he bargained for. His male caretaker, Harrison, tended to get himself into odd predicaments. The Rottweiler was certain that the rattlesnake incident hadn't gone exactly as Harrison said. Freckles was just glad that good old Harry or Rags hadn't been bitten. On the other hand, the dog knew his own personality and probably would have charged right at the snake, as the Saint Bernard had likely done. After all, Rottweilers weren't known for their caution, either.

Case in point: chasing the marten the first time hadn't come out as he expected. And neither did his next encounter—for out of the corner of his eye he saw the rascally marten staring at him from outside the shed.

The second chase was on!

In his hurry, Freckles knocked over the bike to get to the marten, breaking the kickstand in the process. "Freckles!" Harrison yelled, but the dog had already run out the shed door.

This chase didn't last nearly as long as the first. As a matter of fact, it was over before it started. The Rottweiler saw the weasel (or rodent or whatever it was) just in time to see its flippant grin toward the dog, and then it was gone. Freckles circled the area in hot pursuit but could not find the marten anywhere. He had lost its scent, too. Where had it gone?

Harrison stepped out of the shed, "Come here, boy. We'll get that critter, don't you worry." So, his caregiver had seen the marten, too.

Perhaps it would be better if they worked together to address their common foe.

"Look at this, Harry," yelled Lana from the house. "A bunch of hummingbirds have congregated at the bird feeder. It's odd to see so many here at once, especially since all the nectar has been eaten already."

Freckles' ears perked up for a third time. The hummingbirds had returned. He hadn't imagined them. So, he strutted over to say hello.

When they saw him, the seven hummingbirds completely ignored him, preferring to continue circling the bird feeder. At first, Freckles was disappointed. He had thought that they were his friends.

Harrison strode to the bird feeder, and Freckles thought that he would shoo them away. Harrison had only agreed to a bird feeder at Lana's insistence. He wasn't one for decoration, nor was he particularly fond of birds.

He surprised the dog, however. He looked at them as if they were a natural art form. Contrary to his gruff self, Harrison was a lover of paintings, usually depicting history. What he liked about this picturesque scene Freckles could only guess, but he admired it nonetheless.

"Aren't they lovely, flying like that," Lana said. "They are flying in such rhythm and harmony. It's as if they want to show us something." Maybe so, but it wasn't the humans that the performance was for. Freckles watched to figure out what they were attempting to tell or show him.

One hummingbird flew below the bird feeder until it touched the ground slightly with its beak. Then another hummingbird joined the first, circling the land-bound bird and then thrusting with alarming speed back to the bird feeder, like a rocket into space. Freckles had once seen a rocket on the flat box that Harrison was always watching. Ever since, he had wanted to see it again. Perhaps this hummingbird was providing him this image.

"What are they doing?" Harrison asked.

"Don't know," his wife responded. "But whatever it is, it's got to be better than whatever lame-brained idea you were conniving in the shed."

"Didn't I build you that bird feeder?" her husband retorted. "Never get any respect, I tell you," he continued, addressing the dog.

"If you got it right the first ten times, Harry, I'd give you some respect," Lana jibed. Freckles was used to this banter and realized that this was the way that humans interacted lovingly. The Rottweiler preferred sniffing butts, but different species had distinct ways of connecting with each other.

Meanwhile, the remaining birds formed a picture, flying left and right of the thrusting hummingbird, beaks outward, depicting something Freckles was beginning to recognize. They were showing him a tree, but not just any tree; it was the Douglas-fir, where he had gotten stuck after the chase.

"Are they showing us some kind of metaphor?" Lana asked.

"They're just dumb birds. They aren't showing us anything," her husband said.

"They are graceful and beautiful and are in tune with nature," his wife responded. "When was the last time you admired anything in nature?"

"Eh, I'm a builder, not a naturalist," said Harrison.

These two don't get it, the dog thought. But Freckles was on the hummingbird's wavelength. He knew this had something to do with the pine marten, for he and the hummingbirds were joined against the dastardly weasel (or whatever), although the Rottweiler did not yet know what the marten had done against the birds.

The answer came rather quickly, for the bird whose beak touched the ground suddenly rolled over as if it were dead as another hummingbird seemed to attack it. Freckles spoke predator-prey language so understood right away. The marten had attacked one of their own, perhaps beneath the Douglas-fir. The marten seemed to like to trap or catch its prey off-guard at that location.

That's it, Freckles thought. *We will turn the bones on the marten so that it becomes the prey.*

The birds seemed to have that exact sentiment, for the bird that had feigned death rose from the ground and attacked the other hummingbird, who then was the one to fall to depict the marten's demise.

"These birds are funny," Harrison was saying. "They are fluttering all around but not really doing anything. Is this what those birdwatchers do all day, watch nothing?" The old man had had enough and walked back in the house.

The old woman dismissed him with a wave of the hand. "They are lovely—right, Freckles?"

"Woof," he barked in agreement. And Freckles started plotting out his plan for the marten, which would involve these fine hummingbirds, if they were agreeable to it, which they seemed to be.

Chapter 10
Following Each Other

What were they doing after hours? Certainly not construction. The place might be a construction site, but assembling or building was not on the agenda. Could they be doing something illegal? But where was the cocaine, LSD, prostitution ring, stolen material, or even a bong? Weren't big bouncer types supposed to be selling drugs or hoarding stolen goods? For all he knew, these materials could be stolen. But why? He mostly saw these guys sewing garments with pretty flowers embroidered on them. These broad hulky men were wusses stitching clothes instead of carrying gold bars or mounds of coal for rich men, polluters, or pseudo-politicians.

Now don't get him wrong. Hippie liked the clothing. The garments reminded him of peace and love, so foreign in most of today's culture where money ruled all. But that's what confused him so much—where was the money?

Hippie gave up trying to piece out what he was seeing. "What on Mother Earth is going on here?" he asked Maude.

"Can't you see? They're making clothes for Christmas."

"Ummm. But it's huge men knitting in August at a construction site in Lake Tahoe, not elves sewing during Christmas time in Santa's workshop at the North Pole. Can you understand my confusion?"

"They got to do it sometime, somehow," Maude replied.

"Do they?"

"Yeah, for the kids."

"But most of this clothing looks adult-sized." Hippie was starting to think that Maude was just making this up or setting up an elaborate joke, but he decided to play along for just a bit longer.

"Yeah, that's right. Kids come in all shapes and sizes. I'm a kids, you know." Maude looked completely serious.

"Huh?"

"You know, KIDS—Kindred I Deem Spiritual. Not your government agency, for sure. That's why we're working at this late hour at this odd location."

For the first time since he had left his fellow boaters, he questioned his decision to stay with Maude. He was used to and even tolerated spiritual nutcases (see Bearman), but a whole gang of them might be a different story. "What about your delivery?" he thought to ask to see just how far Maude was involved with this group.

"Some of this stuff is in my truck. I also have other goods to peddle, too, and other salespeople to sell everything." Maude jumped out of the truck then and yelled over to a broad hairy man who seemed akin to Bearman, except that he was taller, and one could tell that he was not a bear at first glance. "Frank, bring that sweater over."

"Yes, ma'am," Frank said obediently.

Maude presented Hippie the sweater. "Feel the grainy texture, delicate embroidering, intricate but affordable jewelry, and fine plant cloth. Can't you feel the volcanic glass, petrified logs, precious minerals consisting mostly of emeralds and rare plants?"

"As a man of nature, I think I can," Hippie acknowledged, fingering the coarse plant inner cloth of the sweater. "But how can anyone wear this? It feels like a Navajo blanket laced with opium."

"Yes, Mexican opium or peyote, to be more exact," replied Frank, nodding agreeably, like a two-legged hyena.

Hippie frowned. What were these KIDS into? Drugs? Nature? The underground market? Some kind of peculiar revolt against society? Weird spiritualism? All or none of the above?

Eh, Hippie thought. *Whatever. Let's just go with it.* And that was Hippie's entire disposition in a nutshell.

"We gotta go," announced Frank as he watched the rest of the hulksters dash off with the loot of sewed clothes made from rare substances. Far off, a black ghetto car zipped down the street. It came to a stop at the construction site just as Frank disappeared around the corner.

Hippie expected the person who got out of the vehicle to be some sort of hoodlum. After all, the car was still bouncing on its wheels even after the engine was turned off. However, the person who

Ridicula

climbed out was a woman in a suit and in vogue sunglasses. Of course, she could still be a hoodlum, just a well-dressed one.

"You Aspen?" she questioned, walking right up to him. She took off her shades and stared right at him, like Medusa without the snakes or the death.

"Are you looking for me rather than those men that ran off?" he asked matter-of-factly in return.

"Yep, I have to ask you something."

"Are you a detective? You have the shades for it."

"No."

"Then who are you?"

"Carolyn's the name and info is my game." She sounded like some juvenile reporter from a middle school newspaper. Or someone from Fox News. Or perhaps from CNN or MSNBC. Did it matter anymore? If she started repeating herself a hundred times and calling everything "Breaking News," then she would be a bona fide reporter.

"Is there some breaking news I need to know?" Hippie asked, smirking.

"Need some answers, that's all." She pulled out a picture of a man with a dorky smile and a scraggly beard. "Do you know this man?"

Upon closer inspection, Hippie knew who it was, although the photo was likely an old one. George looked nothing like that picture, at least as of the last time Hippie had seen him. "Just because I'm a hippy, do you think I know every other hippy in this world? I'm not a typical hippy, either. And anyways, you never disclosed who you work for."

"News blog for the Daily Planet. We have a case to break," she replied in a tone more serious but wabblier in utterance than any of the reporters' tone on MSNBC or Fox News.

It figured that she had to break the case. CNN would be proud. Then he thought about the name of the news agency she worked for. It sounded familiar, but he couldn't put his finger on it. "Ya ain't breakin' no cases wit me," he said in the best defiant slang he could muster.

"You know this man, don't you?" the woman pleaded more than asked. She spoke almost knowingly but with a trace of shakiness in her voice.

Maude broke into the conversation. "Get outta here, you dirty reporter!" she yelled, pushing her considerable bulk into the petite woman's body. Although Maude barely touched her, the reporter fell backwards, landing on her skinny butt and needing to balance herself with her hands, like a baby first learning to sit up.

"How dare you?" Carolyn screamed, not attempting to get up. She knew not to face Maude with anything other than words. At least she had that sense, but otherwise, Carolyn seemed totally unhinged, recoiling like a cat trapped in a corner.

"How dare you?" Maude repeated back loudly, as many people do when they argue.

"You've ruined my pants. Now I'll just have to report your numbskulls that just ran off," Carolyn replied and then hesitated. "Are you sure you're not going to tell me where this guy is?"

Maude interfered again. "You know who he is, I think. You're just trying to find him."

"Why?" asked Hippie.

"He's the leader of a cult, and he's got to be exposed." Carolyn found the courage to look up at Maude, but her eyes immediately lowered back down with a whimper.

"Cult? Yeah, right." George would more likely jump off the Brooklyn Bridge than be the leader of a cult.

"Ah, I knew you knew him," Carolyn avowed. "Where is he?"

"Don't know. Guess your trip here was for naught after all." Hippie chuckled. This woman wasn't going to find out shit — just a matter of principle for Hippie. "How did you find me here anyway?"

"Those numbskulls, that's how," the so-called reporter alleged. Her reporter's story wasn't adding up. How could she have spoken with one of those hulksters? They had all run off before she had gotten here.

Angered at the name-calling, Maude was about to wring Carolyn's neck with her foot, probably because of the name-calling, but Hippie stopped her via a goofy unvoiced plea. Decapitating Carolyn wasn't the way to silence someone or the way to discover the truth. At least that was never Hippie's method.

Carolyn rose to her feet then, for Maude had backed up a few steps to give her some breathing room, a much more considerate notion than stepping on her windpipe so that she couldn't breathe. The reporter began to speak but then stopped, preferring to back away toward her car instead. Evidently, she had finally realized that she wasn't going to get anywhere with them.

Hippie called to her, not quite finished with the conversation. "Where are you going? For that matter, where are you from?"

Carolyn kept walking toward her car, off balance, as if possessed by a drunk demon. And she didn't answer his questions. What all this nonsense meant remained a mystery. Except Hippie felt a sudden sense of dread in the air. He couldn't explain it, but it was there nevertheless.

"You know what, Maude? She probably has been following us a long time. Let's turn the tables and follow her." To Hippie this logic made sense, as long as a peaceful resolution could be achieved.

They left the construction site moments after Carolyn, making sure to keep a safe distance behind her. They made it to the main road where Carolyn made a left at a gas station, followed by two more lefts. Maude followed but lost track of her after the third left. "Where is she?"

Hippie was about to shrug but instinctively looked behind instead. Not one hundred feet away, the distinctive black ghetto car was now following them. "I was right. She has been following us and is now doing it again."

Maude sped up and made a bunch of left turns, either rolling through stop signs or going through yellow lights, causing Carolyn to slow down or stop. Eventually, the truck ended up behind the ghetto car. "That will show her," Maude muttered.

But it was now Carolyn's turn to try the left-hand turns. Obviously, she was on to the game and wanted to continue. Why? The jig was obviously up. Was she all there in the brain, or did she just like odd car chases?

Maude pulled into a gas station, the same one they had passed at least once before. That was just fine with Hippie, for he was beginning to feel nauseous and dizzy. It felt nothing like when experiencing niacin, so he wanted the symptoms to end.

The black ghetto car pulled in soon afterward, tires bouncing to a stop and the engine clunking off a moment later. Carolyn stepped out of the vehicle, walking unsteadily as if she had just got off a speeding carousel ride. Hippie felt her dizziness even as his was dissipating.

"Enough of these shenanigans. Where are you off to next?" the reporter asked as she began to walk straighter.

"Don't know," Hippie replied, truly unsure.

"Well, I'm coming with you."

"No, you ain't," answered Maude.

"Yes, I am."

"Un-huh."

"A-huh." Hippie could tell that the dizziness was wearing off, for Carolyn stood totally upright now and her voice was steady.

"Nope," said Maude.

"Yep," replied Carolyn.

Hippie realized that this could go on for a while, so he interceded. "We have no room in the front for a third person."

"Well, you can make room."

"What about your car?"

"That piece of crap can stay here. I'll even leave the keys for some drifter to take it." Carolyn was adamant about coming. Why? Hippie was not sure.

"You're not traveling with us," Maude continued, but she didn't sound convincing. Perhaps the other woman's stubbornness was winning her over.

"Yes, I am coming."

Hippie knew where this would eventually lead. It looked like their little party would grow to three.

Chapter 11
The Send Button

How did we get smack dab in the middle of a cornfield near Youngstown, Ohio, in the middle of the night? Maria asked herself. She never dreamed that she would ever ever ever ask that question.

George. That was the simple answer that Jade would give — that it was all George's fault. But that was not quite fair. Only Jade would see it in such black and white terms, because Jade had a lot to do with it, too. The fact that Jade did not have any shoes and thus had refused to go on the dirty train had been a reason why Maria wasn't sleeping in the comfort of her apartment right now. Why the train was so much dirtier to Jade than all the places she had walked since throwing her sandals onto the highway was beyond Maria's comprehension. Possibly, the real reason for her refusal to go on the train was because she was afraid of it. Jade possessed many phobias, including common ones such as the fear of heights and spiders, but also strange ones, such as the fear of flies and the color orange. Maria would not be surprised if trains were on the phobia list.

In any case, Faulkner had already dropped them off at the Newark station when Jade announced her refusal to get on the train. Instead, she had stayed put in the waiting area while George set off to buy her shoes, insisting that he knew exactly what Jade wanted. Maria had stayed with Jade while Kenny and Bobarino went to get something to eat.

Why they had all stayed behind instead of some of them taking the train was another mystery to Maria until Bobarino returned. "Why are you still here?" she simply asked, eying his and Kenny's burgers and fries while Maria ate a yogurt. Jade did not wish to eat until George came back with her new shoes.

"It's an adventure. I love adventures," he replied. "And also, I'm being paid as if I were on shift until I return the cab. Guess that's not going to happen, but the principle is still the same."

"What am I going back to? I'm not working today and haven't stepped outside the city or its suburbs my whole life," added Kenny. "This is my chance to explore...."

"Even if it is in Jersey," he finished.

Of course, in retrospect, they should have left when they had the chance. But how could they know what would happen?

What did not happen next was George's return. He had said that he would be back in a deadpan Arnold Schwarzenegger voice, but unlike Arnold, George was not true to his words. After about an hour of waiting, the rest of the group became fidgety. When he didn't pick up his phone, they became testy. Finally, Kenny raised his hands and renounced his friend. "Fuck him. Let's just go. If Jade wants to stay behind and wait for him to return with new shoes, she can."

"Screw this," Jade said, somehow daintily. She immediately ran to find a seat on the next train, which had just arrived. Without questioning, they all got on it. Ditching George seemed to be the cure for her fear of going on a train barefoot.

But the cure didn't take. Jade stepped on the train and immediately jumped to the closest empty seat. On the next seat over, an elderly Latin man stared at her like she was a demoness on Earth. "Diablesa pierna desnuda! (Translation: The bare leg of a she-devil!)" he screamed. Maria's description had immediately proved apropos.

The man pulled his necklace from underneath his shirt. Naturally, a cross rested at its base. He held it up and said, "Vete! (Translation: Go away!)"

Jade had no choice but to obey. She stood up, feet on dirty train floor, but immediately fell back when the train moved. She landed directly into the elderly man's arms. Strangely enough, the man didn't say or do anything. Instead he just stared at Jade's feet, possibly in fear, possibly with something else in mind.

Maria helped Jade stand up. "Well, at least we're heading back home," she said.

At that moment, an attendant came on the loudspeaker. "Next stop, Trenton!" They had caught the train going in the wrong direction and had no choice but to wait till Trenton to get off.

Maria sighed at the announcement. She should have figured something like this would happen. What she couldn't figure out was what she saw next, for she recognized the man sitting only three rows in front of her. "What the hell...?"

George turned his head back after hearing her soft Latina voice. "Maria, what a delight! What are you doing on this train?" he inquired.

"I should ask you the same question. Weren't you supposed to be back at the station with Jade's new shoes in hand an hour ago?"

"Couldn't find the right pair. Store said their Trenton warehouse has it in the right size and color and that they could ship it tomorrow."

"So, you are going down to get it?" she asked, flabbergasted. *Did this fool always have to do things the hard way?*

"Didn't any of you get my text message?"

"No!" exclaimed Jade, who had just now realized who Maria was speaking with.

"That's strange," George replied, dumfounded. He looked at his phone, touched a few screens, and blurted out, "Oh, I forgot to press the send button!"

Jade and Maria both shook their heads vehemently at the same time. They were about to let him have it when Kenny and Bobarino cut in.

"And who do we have here?" said Kenny.

"When are we going to replace that cab?" Bobarino asked as if nothing else mattered.

"I'll send you the text now," George said, still looking at his screen, and ignoring the others even though Jade looked like she was about to slug him.

"You're an idiot." Jade stated the obvious, but at least she relaxed her fist and chuckled a bit. Maria had thought George had been serious but perhaps he had been joking.

Maria received a beep on her phone. George's text message read:

No shoes here. Will get them, though. But don't be afraid, Jade. Take the next train home. It won't kill u.

"You're indeed an idiot," Maria said more jovially than she had intended.

In response, a flash of red, yellow, and green light flashed within Bobarino's pocket, as if a tiny alien was trying to escape from his private parts. Then the muzak version of "Greased Lightning" played there, a car exhibition in his pocket.

"At least the car keyrings still work," George said, laughing.

The rest of the train ride went smoothly, if traveling in the wrong direction could be considered smooth. For much of the ride, Jade constantly complained about her bare feet, driving Maria to yell, "Stop with the shoes already!"

Jade took her scream as the warning it was, so in response she created make-do shoes using US Weekly magazine pages and invisible tape. Meanwhile, Bobarino complained about his poor cab being dismantled, and Kenny complained about Bobarino's whining. George seemed content, as if everything was as should be. Maria said hardly another word, for her thoughts centered on what could possibly happen next.

They got off in Trenton, and George insisted on taking a taxi to the shoe warehouse outlet that held Jade's new shoes. At first Bobarino refused to squeeze into the taxi, stating his reason to be that it was too soon; he was still in mourning. He finally gave in when George announced that a free slice of pizza awaited him at the end of the trip.

Bobarino would wait a long time for that slice. As a matter of fact, he still is waiting.

When they got to the shoe warehouse outlet, the manager politely decreed that Jade was not allowed onto the premises because she was wearing magazine shoes, so George went in without her, and Kenny and Bobarino tagged along.

"We'll be back in a moment," George had said, but Maria had instinctively doubted it.

After only a few minutes, Jade could not take waiting any longer and came running into the shoe outlet, tearing off her makeshift shoes in the process. After all, she was in a shoe store where people had to try new shoes on. Maria didn't dare stop her, mainly because she agreed with her friend.

"You said you had the sandals in the right size and color. Now you're saying you can't find them?" George said, exasperated.

"We apologize," uttered the manager to George. And then he saw Jade, and said, "You are not allowed in here unless you buy some shoes immediately to cover your bare feet."

This guy was a piece of work.

Jade loved shoes so much that she had boxes and boxes, and most of them had only been worn once or still divulged the tag on them. Normally she would be happy to buy new silvery taupe pumps, but this manager had rubbed her the wrong way.

And her morals ruled, even when buying shoes.

"You expect me to buy shoes after you stopped me from entering your lowbrow store? Who do you think you are? At the end of the day, you are just a glorified shoe salesman that can't even sell shoes." She then rolled the makeshift *US Weekly* shoes that she still carried into a ball and threw it at the stunned manager. Then, she stomped out (and with bare feet, stomping was a hard thing to accomplish).

Maria and the rest of the group stared after her for a while before following. The manager did not move even after the shoe glossy-paper ball bounced off his forehead.

Maria lay on maize in Ohio reminiscing about all of this. And she continued to muse over the absurdity of the whole situation. After all, everything she recollected thus far had happened before they had left New Jersey. And a lot had happened since then even if it were only a day ago. But her involvement at this juncture in Trenton (although George was still the idiot) was the catalyst for all that happened since, for she was the one to stick out her thumb so that they could get a ride from a wing-nut.

And he drove yet another SUV.

At first, the man seemed cordial enough. He was a young man who looked at her and Jade without any menace or lust. He had a trustworthy appearance: clean-cut, glasses, and wore business attire. He said he was on his way to a meeting but had time to bring them all back to New York City before his meeting began. Maria had neglected to ask what type of meeting it was, though, an oversight that would prove a huge mistake.

Upon settling into the SUV and driving off, the driver said to no one in particular, "Do you guys like movies?" Maria was a little bit perplexed by the question. She hadn't heard of anyone in the free world who didn't like some type of movie. *Next, he might ask, 'Do you like music?' An equally dumb question.*

Of course, George had to answer. "Action movies are the bomb, sometimes literally."

That set off the driver. George tended to say exactly the wrong words to these oddballs, even if it sounded innocent enough. "Those movies are all the same," began the man. "In every movie, the plot and characters always do the same thing. Ever heard of the 'Race & Chase'?"

"Must be the cool car chase that is often a race against time or against each other," George answered. "So, you like those traditional action movies instead of the CGI stuff?"

"How about the 'Run & Gun,' sometimes also referred to as 'Fun with a Gun'?" the man continued, not bothering to answer George's question.

"Oh, that's easy. That's when the protagonist or other character is running through or on top of buildings or war zones or something of the like as the antagonists run after them, shooting wildly."

"How about the 'Fire for Hire'?"

"Hey, that one's clever. A nice switch to being hired then fired at work." George answered excitedly, and Maria instinctively rolled her eyes. "But here you must mean the fire that always starts, often because of car crashes or awesome explosions. In many cases, at least one of the characters is hired to exterminate another character, which ends up a fiery mess."

"Yeah, you know your action movies," said the driver. The words sounded as if they were meant as a compliment, but his disgusted tone said otherwise. "You know of the 'Shot that's Not'?"

"Of course," George answered proudly, missing the sarcasm in the other's voice. "That's when someone is about to shoot someone else, but before he can, something else happens, often someone else shooting, which gives the other time to escape."

Ridicula

"You are good." The driver's disgust was so evident now that even George should have recognized it. "How about 'Said before Dead'?"

"Oh, that's my favorite," George answered, still oblivious to the manner in which the driver was talking. "That's when the man talks forever about his ambitions or plans or how much pain he's going to give the other before killing him. Oftentimes, that gives the protagonist enough time to escape. See every old Batman TV episode ever made." George paused to giggle. "Then," he continued, "there's the other meaning where someone is about to die but must say something, often profound, before he keels over. Am I right?"

"Got them all. So, you must realize how cliché all these movies are?" The driver gave him a sardonic laugh.

"Come on now. They're fun," George replied, possibly finally catching on to the other's attitude.

"You know what really perturbs me about all these action movies?" the driver asked rhetorically as he sped up into traffic. "The way they portray the guns, which seem to be the weapon of choice for the dirty deeds."

Maria didn't like where this conversation was going. Before, the discussion had been somewhat amusing, if a bit sophomoric, but now, she had the feeling that things were taking a bad turn—

Just like the driver was doing now. He had just exited the Jersey turnpike to Route 80 toward Pennsylvania. Maria didn't have a great sense of direction, but that couldn't be right.

"Guns are for protection. They don't kill people. Other people do," the driver continued. Maria had heard this one before. This man might be a gun-toting enthusiast. The thought made a little fear creep up her spine. She looked for any evidence of a gun in the car.

"You see," the man said as the car raced down Route 80, "the Second Amendment says that all men have the right to bear arms. And that is damn right! But glorifying killing with them, that ain't right. I like it when they use other weapons to do the dirty work. Horror movies are better at doing that...."

This man seemed like he was just getting started, so Maria worked up the courage to interrupt him, especially since she didn't see any rifle bags in the car. "I don't think this is the direction back to the city. Where are we going?"

"Where are we going, you ask?" He reached past George and opened the glove compartment. Could there be a handgun in there? "Look at this?"

In his hand was a pamphlet. Maria sighed with relief. She noticed Jade do the same. She seemed nervous, too. The guys were still oblivious to the possibility of danger. *Just like them.*

Her stress quickly returned when she looked at the pamphlet. It read like an ad for the Army, except that it wasn't for the military:

Come see guns, guns, guns, and more! Pistols, rifles, cannons, we got it! Cause the NRA needs you.

While disturbing to her, those words were not what scared her most. These did:

Located in Youngstown, OH.

"Are you taking us here?" Maria asked, already knowing the answer.

"Damn right, I am. You all got to know that guns aren't all bad. You Yankees want them all banned when they can protect you." The man reached into his pocket, so Maria naturally figured that he would pull out a scrunched confederate flag. That's what people like this did.

It was small, one of those toy flags, like what might be found on antipatriotic cake. No matter how tiny, though, it was still a Confederate flag nonetheless.

"I have to go to the bathroom. Pennsylvania is a damn long state. Can you pull over at the next rest stop?" Kenny asked. Had the danger finally dawned on him? Because that was a good idea. They could make their escape then.

"No stops till Ohio. Just pee in a bottle."

"I have to shit," Kenny said, squirming in his seat. Well, that could be bluntly effective.

"This is my father's car. It would serve him right if you crapped in his car." So, the driver had issues with his father. No surprise there.

"I have to go, too," said Jade. "Can't you let a dainty little lady like me have her privacy?" She sounded Southern. Perhaps Jade thought that would persuade this NRA fanatic.

"No!" So much for that.

Everybody went silent, trying to figure out a way to get this guy to stop without causing a horrific accident. Maria thought about what the protagonist in action movies would do in this situation. Perhaps George was thinking the same, for he said, "I just thought of another one. Have you ever heard of the 'Fist with a Twist' in action movies?"

"Can't say I have," the driver responded more jovially than before. "Doesn't sound like anything involving guns."

"You're right," George said as he twisted the driver's arm and attempted to punch him in the face. Meanwhile, Kenny grabbed the steering wheel from the backseat.

In action movies, these events would have led to the protagonist taking over control of the vehicle with the antagonist eventually being thrown out of the car. Unfortunately, in real life, a horrific crash was much more likely. Maria realized this so was relieved when George barely made contact with the driver's face. With no damage done, the NRA fool could still drive, and he did twist free. Afterward, he knocked Kenny's hands from the steering wheel and took it over. "What, are you guys crazy? We could have been killed," the crazy man said ironically. "See, that's what watching action movies gets you. If any of you try anything else, I'll just have to tie you all up." He waved the tiny confederate flag and drove on.

Hours passed with nothing but the driver's ranting. "This is the land of the free. Confederate flags should be bought and swung proudly," he said at one point.

"Why would you want to carry a symbol of the South that reminds us of war and slavery?" George dared to ask.

"I'm a self-respected Southerner," was the driver's answer, as if that explained his entire rationale.

At Ohio's border, Kenny finally couldn't take it anymore. "I'm going right now." He reached for the passenger door handle, threatening to jump out.

"Oh, what the hell. I'll stop," said the driver, but he drove on for quite a while before finally exiting the highway. "Let's take a bathroom break. I could use a soda anyway," he said as they exited. "You all promise to come to the rally. You'll like it. You all will."

"What else could we do in the middle of nowhere?" Jade asked. That was true enough. That didn't mean that they couldn't make a run for it.

They drove until they found an old gas station. They exited the car in front of a crappy convenience store that seemed to have been run down ten years earlier but somehow remained standing. As Kenny ran to the bathroom, Maria could just imagine how disgusting and filthy the toilets must be. She was tempted to try going in the cornfield behind the store but decided to hold it in instead.

"The rally is coming in this direction," a woman yelled running out of the convenience store. "They are bringing it to the people."

The driver who had ungraciously brought them to this place raised his tiny Confederate flag into the air where nobody could tell what it was and announced, "We shall rise again!"

A man next to him examined the tiny flag, squinting so that he could see it better. He did this for many seconds, finally recognizing it. "You're an idiot. The NRA is for guns, not the Confederacy."

"Nevertheless, guns rule!" exclaimed their captor.

To that, the other man smiled in agreement, pulling out his pistol from his gun holster that only now was visible.

"I thought we were in Ohio, not the Wild West," Maria whispered nervously to Jade.

The driver and the man with the handgun gave them little heed, so Maria sauntered behind the convenience store and ran for the cornfield. Jade followed behind. They did not delay seeing if the kidnapper and the man with the gun had noticed them. They were too busy running for their lives.

When a bullet was shot into the air in the anticipation of the rally that could be heard around the bend off a windy dirt road, Maria finally looked back to see that Bobarino and George were catching up to her with great haste. She dove into the cornfield and heard the others do the same. There was still no sign of Kenny. I guess not even a gunshot could scare him from finishing his dump. *He's oddly funny like that, but the guy has a way to grow on you anyway.* Maria somehow blushed at the idea, even though his bowel movements were at the forefront of her thoughts.

So here she was hidden in a cornfield somewhere in Ohio. Maria dared not move as night approached. She would rather spend the night in the relative safety of the cornfield than go anywhere near that rally.

And that is what she did.

Chapter 12
The Hat and the Cat

The pine marten had several names among the animals of the forest, and he was fond of them all. He liked being called Rascally Rascal, because he was doubly mischievous, especially for his species. Martens were generally benign in nature, but he enjoyed causing havoc to those who intruded on his routines or hunts. Another name for him was Nocturnal Nuisance. While not entirely accurate, because he did appear in the day, mostly at dusk or dawn, he was happy to be known as a nuisance since other animals would leave him alone due to his temperament. His favorite name, however, was MOOC—Marten Out Of Control. Of course, those names were perpetuated by the rodents and rabbits of the forest so were not from real credible sources. Nevertheless, his reputation preceded his true nature.

But the dog hadn't received word; otherwise, the rather large pooch wouldn't have interrupted his hunt, forcing MOOC to mock the beast when it got stuck in the tree. Curious about who this dog was and a little perturbed by the loss of his meal, the marten had followed it back to its home and had been keeping tabs on it since. MOOC had a feeling that more games were to be played soon.

In the meantime, the marten carried on, bullying or flat out eating the small rodents, but today it was a cat that had his attention. Normally he would stay away from cats because they were mean critters, for they would torture their prey before killing them. MOOC was never THAT mean. However, this cat had come from the canine's home, so the marten wanted to mess with it.

"Wife, where's my hat?" the old man said, following the cat out.

"It's Lana, Hubby," a creaky but strong woman's voice called. "And it's right where it always is—on the hook next to the door."

"Don't you think I would have seen it if it was there?"

"Try the next hook over."

"Oh, I got it," said the man who probably couldn't see a rabbit if it jumped right in front of him.

"You left the door open, Harry, and now the cat is out again," the woman announced. She was more observant than most humans but not even close to the marten's level, for he had already seen the cat climb up the shed. Perhaps it was time to give it a little scare.

Rascally Rascal crept toward the shed, trying not to let the cat see him. Cats were keen when they were awake, so this movement was a careful process. As he approached, he wondered where the dog was. He did not want that ignoramus clod messing up his fun. Although the dog had no love for the kitty, the marten still thought the Rottweiler would aid the cat against a common foe, which of course would add to the fun.

Meanwhile, the cat settled on the roof of the shed, attempting to bask in the early morning sun. All cats loved to sleep, and this one liked to do it in the sun, as the marten had seen plenty of Cymric cats do. Since it was so inclined to sleep at the moment, sneaking up to it would be easier. He crept closer.

"Where are you going?" the old woman asked.

"Have to get something from the shed," the old man replied, oblivious to most everything that was going on.

At the base of the shed, Rascally Rascal began to climb right under the cat's nose. Boy, would it be in for a surprise!

He reached the roof, only inches from where the cat soundly slept. He jumped on the roof tile, far enough out of the way to avoid the cat's claws but close enough to jolt it awake. The cat jumped up and screeched. Seeing MOOC, it hissed menacingly, but the marten only gave his rascally grin. Scared, the cat jumped from the roof of the shed—

And onto the old man's hat!

Now, a cat on a hat was simply hilarious to the marten, especially since the old man didn't realize that anything had happened until the cat swiped at the hat with its claws, unintentionally scratching the man's bald head. The elder yelped like a mouse being toyed with by a cat. As fitting an end as that could be, the hilarity was not finished, for the cat slid off the bald man's head with the hat still intact on the cat's claws. Both cat and hat flew like a kite with no wind, so fast they skidded to the ground with the cat's claws tearing the hat to bits. So there went the skittish cat with the torn hat.

"What have you done with my hat, you stupid cat? That's my favorite hat." The man still smarted from the scratch on his head but became angrier when he saw that his hat more resembled a dead plant than something to be worn on his head. He lurched angrily around like a two-legged dog without a bone or a clue.

In that instant, the large dumb dog scrambled out of the house like a moving log, barking nonstop. He was looking straight up at MOOC.

"What is it, Freckles? That's not like you barking like that."

That dog's name is Freckles! How ridiculous! Somehow, the marten would eventually let him know just how ludicrous that name was for that type of dog.

The dog that had no freckles continued to bark and stare in the marten's direction. Well, even a dimwitted human could eventually figure out where the dog was looking. Thus, while this whole affair had been fun, the marten knew when it was time to leave. He gave the dog his trademark rascally grin and disappeared behind the shed and then back into the woods, where he could wait until night when the mischievous Nocturnal Nuisance would return.

Freckles lost sight of the marten and was about to start scenting and chasing when Harrison called to him. "Whoa, boy, stop! We don't want you going off on a wild goose chase just now. We have some important work to do today."

Freckles debated chasing the wily weasel anyway but remembered how his past encounters hadn't gone as planned. He was in the process of plotting his next encounter and did not want to rush anything, especially since he now might have another ally to work with.

He had seen what the marten had done and thought that only he should be able to scare the cat when he deemed fit. Thus, this once, he entertained the notion of an alliance with a cat. He trotted over to where the cat was still trying to disengage from the hat.

"Pebbles, haven't you done the hat enough damage?" asked Harrison, still trying to calm himself, for the hat had meant a lot to him for some reason, though Freckles could not understand why. The hat was large and fitted him like a rug on his head. Perhaps that was the reason. Humans had strange body issues, and Freckles had heard that baldness was a major one. The dog could understand that one. He imagined being without fur and saw himself as a large hairless Khala. On the outside, he only snickered, but internally he laughed uproariously.

When his thoughts returned to vengeance on the marten, he continued his trot towards the cat. But communicating with Pebbles wasn't always the easiest. Sure, they understood each other when it came to food, chasing, and sleeping. When both wanted food, they begged for it, although the cat was less direct about it. Pebbles may feign that she was not interested, but when push came to shove, the meowing started. As for chasing, there was an order: Freckles chased Pebbles, and the cat ran. She could chase something smaller than her, but that was of little concern to the dog. As for sleeping, as long as the cat was not in his space, she could sleep where she wanted. Pebbles understood that Freckles' part of the kitchen was only for him as was his beanbag and blanket. Other communication took more doing, however, for his barks were mostly only noise rather than speech to the ears of humans and cats. Thus, Freckles had to contemplate how he could communicate his plans to the cat about the pine marten.

"Instead of destroying my hat, why didn't you go after that rascally weasel?" Harrison asked the cat. "That critter's eating my blueberries, bothering my pets, and wreaking havoc. We've got to do something, don't we? My trap will work, won't it?"

Pebbles did what most cats would do when asked those questions: lick itself. However, Freckles saw understanding in the cat's eyes, which gave the dog an idea: he could communicate with the cat through the human. But how could he get Harrison to tell the cat the plan?

What a dilemma!

Well, Freckles was a smart dog. He could figure this out.

Naturally, the first thing he tried was to bark. Harrison spun agitatedly toward the dog. Pebbles forgot about the shredded hat and ran away. Obviously, that tactic didn't work.

Then he thought to wag his tail playfully. Sure enough, Harrison reacted. "What'cha want, boy? Wanna play fetch?"

Freckles ran towards the cat, who had just scampered behind some bushes a few meters away. Of course, the old man threw the stick the opposite direction, ruining the dog's plan to bring the cat and the man together.

When Freckles did not fetch the stick, Harrison lost interest. So much for that plan.

The dog had one more idea. He raced off and scratched on the window to be let back into the house. Lana obliged, but instead of going inside, Freckles waited, whimpered while pointing his head toward the old man, and started trotting back over to him.

"What did he do now?" Lana asked the dog. Freckles kept walking, and she followed. So far so good.

"What are you doing, Husband?"

"The cat destroyed my hat, all because of that weasel thing," Harrison started, obviously perturbed and still a bit frantic. "We got to get that weasel for eating my blueberries and making Pebbles tear my hat."

Lana rolled her eyes, a motion the dog saw often when she was talking to her husband. "Yeah, have you figured out how you are going to do that yet?" she asked, obliging him as she usually did.

"My trap—"

Freckles didn't wait for Harrison to continue, for the human's plan was flawed at best. Instead, the Rottweiler whined for their attention and trotted toward the cat. Lana, the sharper of the two humans, heard him and started toward him with Harrison slowly following—what the old man had planned to say had been forgotten.

"Did Pebbles do something?" Lana asked.

"Yes, my hat—" Harrison began, and the cat remained where she was.

Thus, a conversation of sorts began. Freckles had a long tedious process ahead of him but communication was started. Eventually, however, Freckles, by involving all of them in the communication, would make these dullards understand his plan. He would prance and dance, whine and doggy sign, and move his paw until they understood what they saw.

After that, Freckles would let the hummingbirds in on the plan, which he was sure would be easier since birds had a better understanding of how to converse animal to animal than a cat or man ever would. Birds and dogs simply understood each other's movements and gestures while cats ran when a dog came close and men were, well, human.

But when all was said and done, and the plan was ready for action, then that marten had better watch out!

Chapter 13
A Soap Altercation

To say that Hippie was a man of little means was like saying that Donald Trump is a bullheaded narcissistic billionaire president. In other words, the statement was more than just the truth: it was just the way of it. So, when Carolyn offered him money, he kindly declined. "That's all right. I don't need anything much—just some food and drink, the clothes on my back, and an occasional covering over my head."

"You stink!" said Carolyn. "You make Maude here smell like sweet petunias."

They had been on the road for a few hours, heading east. Carolyn had mostly been quiet, sensing some tension coming from Maude's aura, but she must have whiffed something not to her tastes that had caused her outburst. Still, Hippie had heard that an oversensitive nose could be associated with mental disorders, especially when the smell was something different or nonexistent. That fitted Carolyn's mode, because she was definitely not all there. He had been suspicious of that when they met, which only strengthened as he got to know her better.

Most people might be offended by that comment, including Maude, but Hippie just shrugged. "So, you don't like the smell of nature even though you mention flowers. So be it."

"Maybe something from Nature's Soap would be fine, but what you smell like is dreadful." Carolyn pinched her nose and cowered near the window.

"If you don't like it, you can get out. I don't even need to stop the car. We can just open the door and push you right out. I wouldn't mind hearing some of your bones crunch as you roll down the shoulder of the road," said Maude, still needing to warm up to Carolyn's nutty charms. Not everyone was as easygoing as Hippie.

"Now, now, there's no need for that," he said to Maude. "If you don't like the odor of the plants I use for deodorant, we can stop off for some of that Nature's Soap you just talked about. I'm not one to take money, but suitable gifts are always welcome."

"Are you sure that we shouldn't just toss her out? We can get rid of her at the Humboldt Wildlife Park and dump her in the wetlands. The rangers probably wouldn't find her for weeks, and the coots could have at her," said Maude. Hippie thought that she might be serious.

"Nah," and Maude took his demur to heart. Most of the time people tended to abide by what he wanted. He thought that perhaps it was his Jesus persona that influenced them, like it did Bearman, even though he certainly was not the religious icon.

"Well, then we better get that soap then, or this suit won't stop gabbing about it."

"A souvenir shop at Humboldt should have something," Carolyn declared, seemingly unruffled by Maude's comments.

"Wouldn't a convenience store or something be easier?" Maude asked.

"You see one around here?" retorted Carolyn. Route 80 went on and on without an exit in sight.

"Don't worry. I know the lay of the land. I'll find one. Just brace yourself." At 80 MPH, Maude pulled off the highway and onto the shoulder where a bent railing awaited. The truck slightly caromed off it but mostly plowed through it and into a ditch, where the tires bounced on like a kickball. Beyond lay open land with dirt and occasional hovels rather than road and plaster.

"What the—" began Carolyn but a bump made her grab her seatbelt for safety rather than finish her expletive.

"Oh, this is going to be fun," Hippie announced, meaning it.

The truck bounced and rattled like a snake on a trampoline as Maude maneuvered around trees and over dirt, rocks, and hills. This close to Humboldt, the terrain was not as deserted as other areas of Nevada, making the ride like a bumper car on a roller coaster. Hippie moved with every turn and bounced like a horseback rider with every bump. He lived for the adventure and danger. He almost drifted into Sporting Aspen mode with the adrenaline but loved the nature around him too much to convert, for Hippie was just being his true self.

Ridicula

Carolyn, on the other hand, looked as if much of her innards were about to release from her. Her face shone a bright red and her eyes went wide with her mouth open. Her hair flew in every direction, but her arms were still, for the air conditioning and her own fear provided the only wind in the truck's cabin. But to her credit, she never did puke onto her fancy suit.

The ride was over all too quickly for Hippie when the truck smacked its way onto a little-used road miles from the Humboldt National Forest. Directly ahead of them a few buildings could be seen, one being a conveniece store and gas station. "Told you I'd find a place that has some soap for sale," said Maude with proud satisfaction.

Her face beginning to lose its reddish hue, Carolyn found her voice. "Haven't got the soap yet."

They arrived at the store, and all exited the truck in search of the soap. The women entered the store, but Hippie lagged behind. He just had a hunch that he should wait for them outside. Shortly afterward, a pickup truck came roaring up to a halt right beside him.

Hippie couldn't believe who the driver was: Bearman. What a coincidence!

This time, Bearman was alone. The two men that Maude had pummeled was not with him. Hippie wished those boys good health. That's the kind of guy he was.

"Jesus, you've returned," Bearman announced, immediately recognizing him.

"Come here to pick up soap." Hippie had decided not to correct him. There was no use trying.

"I haven't washed in days," said the hairy Jesus disciple. "I will heed your advice and lather up at the next truck stop." The image of Bearman in a shower disturbed Hippie, but he did not show it, for Jesus would not have such scorn. After all, all men were created in his image. Thus, they all showered beautifully, bare-skinned and hairy and all.

"Is there anything you need of me?" Bearman asked.

"Clean and be well is all I ask," Hippie replied.

Bearman bowed. Guess that's what he thought would be the best thing to do. Perhaps he thought Jesus was also an emperor.

"You'll never believe this," Carolyn said, coming out of the store. "They actually have the soap, Nature's Best."

Hippie smiled and waved his hand like a magic wand as he said, "Your wish is my command."

Bearman raised his head from his bow and immediately saw Carolyn. Hippie noticed him look at her a little too long, a glint apparent in his eyes, all of his features frozen as if time had stopped for him. Had Hippie just witnessed "Love at First Sight" or just two people akin to crazy?

"Are you my goddess?" Bearman asked her. His sudden conversion to paganism aside, he was certainly immediately enthralled with her, for that question could not be just a stupid pickup line.

Weirdly enough, Carolyn seemed to enjoy this man's candor. "I may be."

Bearman smiled. "Well, Jim is at your service forever, lovely creature! I will protect you." Jim took something from his jacket, or perhaps just from his chest of hair. It was a gun, but unlike last time, Hippie could tell immediately that it was a toy gun. Earlier, he had not seen the red spots painted on what was obviously plastic if seen from up close. Jim squirted water into the air to show mock protection of Carolyn.

Unlike the bumpy truck ride, this talk was making Hippie's innards rumble in disgust. He was not one for corny sentimentalism. His sentiment was always real.

"Oh, Jim, I may have other use for you yet," Carolyn said, implying something other than protection.

Hippie did not like this kind of talk either, and said so: "He may be a bear of a man and a bit whacko, but he is not your toy no matter how beautiful he thinks you are."

"Oh, I was only joking. I will not mistreat him, you Jesus clone!" She must have heard the earlier conversation. "I have more important people to mistreat anyway!"

Jim or Bearman (Hippie still preferred the latter) was not listening to the conversation. He kept on watching Carolyn—so enamored was he that he did not want to lose sight of her for one moment. Finally he blinked, which broke his trance, at least enough for him to talk again.

"I dreamed of a goddess to set foot in front of me, dressed in a suit with brunette bun hair and a petite nose. But little did I know that you'd be blessed by Jesus himself, too." So he had taken Hippie's fake magic wand motion as a blessing. *That figured.*

Maude exited the store by somehow slamming the door open, for the door hit the wall in back of it like a drunk swinging open a beer-loaded refrigerator. "You were supposed to buy this, girl. You owe me," she said, waving a box of Nature's Best soap at Carolyn.

Unabashed by Maude although he recognized her, apparent by the way his eyes twitched, Bearman walked right up to her, grabbed the box of soap, and replaced it with a twenty. "Thank you. I'll be needing this soap at the truck stop."

Maude's mouth dropped. She had been anticipating a sarcastic reaction from Carolyn, not a thank-you from an overly hairy man. Silent for once, she walked right back into the store to buy another box of soap with the twenty.

Meanwhile, Bearman addressed Carolyn again. "Stay here, my beauty, and I will return for you. I will be cleanly washed and ready to court you." And just like that, he entered his truck and drove off.

"Umm, we won't be waiting for him," Carolyn announced, clearly not enticed by anything Bearman might offer. "When Maude returns, we go."

"But don't you find him cute?" Hippie teased. "And anyway, didn't you say that you had use for him? I'm sure he'd be obliging." He added a lewd tongue gesture for effect.

Carolyn giggled. "Oh, forget that. Let's just go."

They waited for Maude, but when she didn't come outside for several minutes, Carolyn became restless and charged into the store. Hippie shook his head but followed, knowing that whatever came next might get ugly if he didn't stop the incident from happening.

"You take that long to get soap?" Hippie heard Carolyn yell.

"What is it to you? You should be paying anyway. Not your boyfriend, Jim." Maude's voice was surprisingly calm, but Hippie knew that might not last.

"Give it here," Carolyn countered, seeing that Maude had the soap.

"Not till you pay your share, and I'm not talking about the soap."

"I have money in your truck, I think. Or did I leave it in my car?" Even to Hippie, Carolyn seemed unconcerned about where her money was.

"Oh, you're not gonna try that, girl." Maude's voice was rising, and crude talk would follow.

Hippie decided to intercede. "Now, ladies," he began.

Carolyn turned to him with a nasty gaze. "Oh, shut up! Why aren't you paying?"

"Wait a second, didn't Bearman or Jim or whatever his name is already pay with that twenty?"

"Yeah, for the first box of soap," Maude chimed in.

"How much does this stuff cost?"

"Oh, plenty. It's Nature's Best." This wasn't like Maude. Hippie hadn't had to pay for much of anything so far for this trip. That was a good thing, because all he had was a dollar thirty-three worth of change in his pants.

But the questions remained: why did Maude want money now? Why did she suddenly need Carolyn to pay her way?

"If neither you nor Hippie have the money, then I guess I'll take the soap and my truck and be off without you." Hippie didn't immediately know who Maude was addressing until she asked him, "Aspen, are you coming?"

Before he could answer, Carolyn ran past him and out of the store.

"Good riddance," said an almost elated Maude. Hippie could now be somewhat certain that this wasn't about money, not that he thought about attaining money much.

"Don't count your blessings. Your truck door is open." They watched as Carolyn jumped into the passenger's seat."

"Oh, no, she fuckin' don't," Maude said in a way unbecoming even for her.

"Now, we can work this out," Hippie interjected.

But Maude stomped over to her truck anyway. "You ready to be twisted into a bitch pretzel?" she screamed at Carolyn.

This was not good. Not good at all.

Carolyn shut the truck door and locked it from the inside. Of course, this didn't stop Maude, who had a key, but it did give Hippie enough time to run over and shove his body between Maude and the door. "Stop right now!" he yelled as loudly as he thought he should, which was hardly loud at all because of his pacifist manner.

"She's got something coming to her, this one." Maude spoke loudly, but her voice didn't come across as a scream. She simply pushed him out of the way and fumbled for her keys.

"Just pay for some gas, Carolyn," Hippie said just loud enough for her to hear.

"No, I won't. There's too much gas here anyway, because you both stink. And she don't need it or deserve it." Hippie had to give it to her. Carolyn was holding her ground even in the face of being contorted into a pretzel.

"You don't need to do this, Maude," Hippie said, appealing to her tender side.

"I don't need to, but I sure want to, so I will." She laughed gruffly as she opened the passenger door and watched Carolyn scramble to the other side.

"You can't escape unless you leave the truck," which was Maude's intention anyway. There really was no need to hurt Carolyn if she left through the driver's side and remained away from the truck.

Maude reached for the smaller woman, but Carolyn still held her ground, if in a bit cowardly manner. Thus, Maude grabbed her and dragged her out of the truck. Carolyn could not thwart her. Maude was just too strong.

Hippie could watch no longer, so he closed his eyes. Maude would make good on her pretzel threat. He could almost hear the crunching of Carolyn's body already, and that disgusted him. Perhaps it was better to see the mutilation than to hear it.

Before opening his eyes, however, he heard a honking sound. At first he thought Carolyn honked the truck horn in desperation, but the horn was coming from a different direction.

Hippie looked that way and saw that Bearman had returned. The horn was a warning, as his pickup was barreling down on where Maude and Carolyn struggled. Maude immediately let go, and an instant later, the pickup came screeching to a halt.

"What, are you crazy? You could have gotten us all killed, including your precious soulmate, or whatever you think she is," Maude yelled after Jim jumped out of his vehicle to escape Maude's fury.

When he was a safe distance away, Jim announced, "I'm now clean and smell great! That soap is a wonder! So now the goddess can travel with me!"

"Good riddance," replied Maude.

"Where am I going?" Carolyn asked, recovering from whatever hurt Maude had already inflicted.

"Why, where Jesus goes, I go. We will follow them." Bearman was smiling now, but he was serious. Hippie could tell, though, by her obvious disgust, that Carolyn had no intention to go to Jim's truck at the moment.

"What?!" Hippie, Maude, and Carolyn yelled at the same time.

Nevertheless, the soap altercation had led to adding a new person to their improbable posse.

Chapter 14
Inside a Jules Verne Novel

Even when she was a young girl, Jade had always been fascinated with shoes. This fascination had often gotten her into all sorts of trouble. When she was only five, she had played with her mother's slippers. At first, she just tried them on. Then she became bolder and decided to dance in them. Her tiny feet tapped and pranced but then kicked a slipper right at the dog's snout. The dog yelped and bit the slipper. Of course, that's when Mommy walked into the room. Since she still danced in the other slipper, Jade had been caught in the act and had been punished.

From there, her obsession increased. She couldn't stop playing with her mother's shoes. She liked the way they felt or looked or sparkled, so she had to get a closer inspection or try them on. Since she never ended up putting them back where she found them, she continued to get in trouble when Mommy could not find one shoe or another.

When she reached the age in which she could buy her own shoes, she did so in bulk. Shoe after flip-flop after heel, she bought and bought until she owed too much on credit and couldn't pay it back. But even this wasn't enough of an incentive to stop buying them. She had to watch her credit card be cut with scissors by a malevolent manager, who thought it funny to do it in front of other customers when it was confirmed that Jade had gone over her limit. Hence, her credit was poor due to her large shoe collection, many of which she had only worn once or never at all.

Yet, that still didn't stop her obsession. Occasionally, a pair of shoes was displayed that she just couldn't resist. Since she didn't have the money to pay for the designer shoes, she stole them. The first few times she did this she wasn't caught, but then her luck ran out when an employee saw her try on the shoes and try to walk out with them on. The store did not take shoplifting lightly, so she ended up in jail for a night. However, she got a break because the judge did not prosecute her further. Still, her obsession continued. Although she had learned her lesson about stealing, she still could not stifle her love for shoes and often still bought on sites, such as ShoeDazzle and Zappos, when she had a little money to spare.

Even with all those incidences of shoe impropriety, she never would have expected her fascination with shoes to get her into the mess she and her friends were in now. The irony of it, though, was that the mess had started because she had thrown a fantastic pair of sandals at a car. For the first time in her life she had sacrificed her shoes, and bedlam had happened as a result.

Still shoeless, Jade crawled out of the corn, her home for the night, more tired than a horse pulling a carriage for weeks on end. She felt like slime, she smelt like Sunday morning Amish fertilizer, she positively looked a wreck, which the most elegant of shoes couldn't fix, she could hear the dirt infesting her very being, and she could taste every one of the aforementioned. In other words, Jade was not a happy woman.

When she got into one of these moods, the person she would complain to was George, who was usually the one to put her in that mood anyway, come to think of it. No wonder she had broken the relationship off. "It's your fault," she said to him even though she couldn't see him.

George crawled out of his section of the cornfield. "Whatever you say, Jade," he acknowledged, even though she really could have been talking to anyone in the group.

Kenny emerged at about the same time as George. "Did you see that thing last night?"

"Crop circles?" asked George.

"Aliens," declared Jade.

"Big Foot," Maria avowed. She was already standing up, dusting herself off. Jade was impressed, for her tresses still lay in a flawless alignment, while Jade's hair was surely matted and frizzy, looking like it was barbecued by the sun in hell.

"Yes, Big Foot is an alien who must have been transported to one of those crop circles. Did you hear it howling?" Kenny always thought he saw aliens or the like, so this conversation was hardly a surprise to

Jade, which was another, but not the biggest, reason she had broken up with George: oddball friends.

"I thought it was the Abominable Snowman," Jade joked, thinking that Kenny would say that they were the same beast.

"Hardly—he doesn't exist," the big goof replied instead. "And if he did, he wouldn't be living in this warm climate."

Jade decided not to press him. She certainly did not want to hear his reasoning of why Big Foot existed while the Abominable Snowman did not. That could only bring on an earful of nonsense.

She was saved from Kenny explaining his ludicrous theory, because Maria interjected, "Oh yeah, let me hear about it." When he turned to say more to her, Jade had that moment to escape. *Thank you, friend for life, Maria!*

Mr. Kenny Dunz had a plan. Not a good one. Possibly not even a sane one. But he had one nonetheless. And it was a simple three-point plan:

1) Borrow a cell phone somewhere since his phone had no battery life, call into work, and say that he was taking all his vacation days immediately, especially since there was little to no chance of his getting back to New York City by tomorrow. If his boss didn't like it, so what? What was the worst that could happen? That he'd get fired from a horrible job? He still had plenty of inventory for his side work of eBay selling anyway.

2) His journey through America would involve his friends new and old. How hard would it be to convince them? They were in the middle of nowhere with him—very far away from their life back home.

3) During their remaining time together, he would put on his admittedly goofy charm for the spicy Maria. He was beginning to really like her. A lot! And he sensed that she liked him, too. After all, she had listened to his talk about Big Foot, and he was aware that that discussion was not for everyone.

The details of his plan were very sketchy at best, except for a piece of luck he had encountered, which the others did not know about. He had unwittingly walked down a different road while hatching up his dynamic plan and had therefore lost his friends temporarily. This was especially stupid on his part because the road was the only turn off they had seen, and he had become lost anyway. So when he came back from his deep thoughts, he was alone, right in front of a car rental place—

If one could call it that. The place lodged a Chevy Cavalier and a Ford Taurus—both looking like good rentals—and the largest SUV Kenny had ever seen: an old beat-up 1970's Chevy Suburban. That was it. There were no other cars on the lot. He did see antique gas pumps, but they must not be operational. Plus, the edifice that functioned as the office was a literal shack, a wooden hole in the wall that may have been built in the eighteenth century. He also spotted a dilapidated sign out front that read, "Tom's Rentals". He half-expected to see Thomas Jefferson step out at any moment, ready to steer the Chevy Cavalier like a motorized horse on his way to sign the US Constitution, which incidentally, Mr. Jefferson never did sign, a piece of trivia that Kenny was proud to know. Instead, however, an older man with a crappy hairpiece opened the door for Kenny.

"You, there! Are you real? Haven't seen anyone this way the whole day. Those racist gun-toting bastards went the other way. Are you one of those asses, wandering around stirring up trouble in these parts?"

Kenny noticed the rifle at the man's side but did not dare bring up that irony. "Ah, no," the normally talkative Kenny said.

"Then what the hell are you doin' on my property?"

"Renting a car?"

The man laughed like a cough. "Are you dull or something? Why the hell would I rent cars here where no one is? I've never rented cars here. That sign is one I've kept since 1974, and the pumps are collectibles."

"Oh, then sorry to bother you," Kenny spoke hurriedly trying to leave unceremoniously, as he didn't want the old man to raise his gun as if he were in the Wild West.

"You've got money?"

"A little," Kenny Dunz admitted without thinking.

"Well, a little will do," the bald man with the modern headpiece stated as he leaned on his gun.

***

Maria was the first to notice that Kenny was missing. How he had gotten that way was a mystery since they were walking on a barely traveled road with little else, besides farmland and open terrain. Where then could he have gone? She couldn't help but feel anxious about his whereabouts.

George, who was the one she'd expect to be missing again, asked, "Kenny, do you have a bottle of water left in your pack?" This was when he noticed that his friend was nowhere in sight.

Jade and Bobarino walked on, still unaware. Jade was concerned only with her bare scratched-up feet. Bobarino stared into the sky as if he were waiting for something miraculous from heaven to happen.

Then something far from miraculous did happen: an SUV drove towards them. However, it wasn't just any SUV: it was the oldest, junkiest, hugest monstrosity Maria had ever seen, short of a monster truck or a gas-guzzling Hummer. It puffed smoke from its exhaust, blew steam from its engine, and sounded like a hyena in heat. When it arrived, she noticed that the paint had been replaced entirely by rust, and the interior had few cushions left to even feign comfort. In other words, it was a step down even from George's horrific cab. Still, the huge car somehow ran and could fit nine, enough room for all four passengers and a small sofa, which Maria was wishing for about now.

And to little surprise, she saw who was driving it: Kenny, of course. He yelled out, "Now we have wheels for the rest of our journey across America!"

Maria had to laugh. She bet that Kenny thought that he had saved the day!

And why not? At this point, Maria would just go with whatever journey awaited. She suspected that the others would acquiesce to further adventure, maybe even want more craziness. All except for Jade, but she would have no choice but to come along for the bumpy ride.

As for Maria, she enjoyed the company, and so far, the misadventures had proved harmless. *So, let's let it ride on!*

***

Jade knew that there would be more trouble after she heard Bobarino announce, "I was exploring at first light and saw a man with a balloon on the other side of the road."

Oh my, what now?

To Jade's surprise, Kenny's "new" Chevy Suburban SUV lasted all the way until they reached a place called Big Sky, Montana, where it stood unable to start up in a parking lot of the latest dive diner where she had just eaten a greasy, fatty hamburger that her stomach could barely digest. The fact that the car had lasted days instead of minutes astounded her. They had stopped along the way to not only eat but also for rest stops, hotels, and to see various sites from Ohio to Montana. Jade had to admit that if not for this spontaneous trip, she may have never been able to see the beginnings of the Old Oregon Trail and the presidential faces of Mount Rushmore and then traveled through the Black Hills and the wondrous Devil's Tower on the way to Billings, Montana. Afterward, they had traveled to Bozeman where Kenny had wanted to head north to see "scary ghosts at the Old Montana State Prison," but common sense had prevailed, and they had gone south toward Yellowstone Park instead.

And yes, she had finally settled on some cheap flats to wear. Her feet had found some reprieve.

But it had looked like their adventures had come to an end with the demise of Kenny's SUV. They had already called a mechanic, who had generously said that he would tow it and give Kenny $35 for ownership of the vehicle, which he would salvage for parts with the rest of the "car" completing its rust-off in a junkyard, where it belonged. Kenny had agreed to this sale. After all, he had only paid for it with $72.53, an inexpensive watch, and a PEZ dispenser for the title. He hadn't even bothered to change the license plates or the registration yet, which was likely illegal, but that would all be taken care of now.

However, Bobarino offered a possibility for more adventure, one that Jade did not like but was intrigued by, nonetheless. She looked at him, interested but pretending like she was perturbed. "A man holding a balloon, huh. Did you throw a dart at it or something?"

"You know, the big balloon," Bobarino lamely explained.

"Oh, like the ones from the Jules Verne novels?" George asked with excitement. At first, Bobarino looked blankly at him, but then he nodded, so George continued, "Where? Where?"

Bobarino pointed in a general direction, and George hopped off that way like a frenzied bunny. George was like that: he often acted like a big kid, which to Jade was both an attraction and a turnoff. She liked his innocent and fun demeanor but disliked his naiveté and his tendency to find himself in ridiculous or even dangerous situations; hence, the main reason for all her recent upheaval.

Of course, the big lug Kenny chased after his friend. When the others followed, Jade reluctantly went as well, although she could feel the terrain beneath her cheap flats as she ran after them.

"Ow- ow- ow," Jade grimaced with every stride she took. She walked on grass but seemed to find a pebble or stick with each step. She watched her feet as she walked but still stepped in a place where she felt the pricks. *For love of better shoes!*

Because of her discomfort and slow pace, she lagged way behind the others. When Maria waited for her, she was thankful at first. Then she realized that they could no longer see the boneheaded males ahead. That meant that they were likely getting themselves into trouble.

"Can you go find those clowns?" she asked Maria. "I'll be all right. These flats do offer a little protection. I will catch up to you. "

"Are you sure?" Maria asked with concern. She really was a good person with a big heart. If they had to be in constant gargantuan messes, she was glad Maria was with her.

"Yes. You've got to stop whatever idiocy those three bozos are probably getting into as we speak."

Maria gave her a knowing laugh. "How did we get here anyway?" The question was rhetorical, for Maria took off looking for the men without waiting for an answer.

Jade stopped walking then. Her feet were killing her. She realized that the blisters she attained before acquiring the flats were the main reason for her discomfort. *Oh, shoes! Throwing away quality sandals all those days ago. What was I thinking?*

The sun slowly rose in blue skies and beat down on her with ever more strength. After not moving for another moment, she realized she would not be able to stand still too much longer without beginning to feel the heat of the morning. Thus, grimacing, she walked, bearing the pain that came with each blistering step.

Jade found her friends hovering around a balloon in the distance. A handwritten cardboard sign with large black letters stated that they were at a BALLOON PORT, although there was only one balloon there now.

What were those asses doing now? Trying to buy the balloon? Jade hoped Maria was talking some sense into those guys.

"Ow, ow, ow," she yelped as she ran across rocky terrain. When she reached a grassier area, she purposely stepped into a small puddle for relief from sun and blisters, flats and all, possibly a first for her since she usually went out of her way not to get any shoe she wore from getting wet or dirty.

Muddied, she kept going until she could finally see what her friends were doing. Unsurprisingly, George and Kenny stood underneath the hot air balloon, holding down the basket while Bobarino and a small mustached man, who could have been Bobarino's sidekick at a circus, seemed to be guiding them on what to do, from inside the basket. Above his mustache, the pilot donned goggles and gloves. Then he turned on the propane gas and watched as the burner came to life, and the frame remained steady, as the pilot dictated.

"You guys are insane!" Maria shouted.

"You got any better ideas?" George replied.

"How about taking a bus?"

"Come if you want. We're going," George said, and he and Kenny climbed in the basket. Their release of the basket also signified liftoff, for the air balloon rose off the ground.

At first, Jade thought about how ridiculous the boys were being. They obviously wanted to travel on the balloon. They probably thought it would be fun, damned the consequences. But then she looked at her poor, blustered, filthy feet and then back from where she had come. No truck, tractor, or pushcart had appeared in all this time.

She doubted if much of anything ever came this way. How was she to get back to civilization in her current walking condition?

Thus, when she reached them she held her arms up high so that she could be lifted into the basket. All this travel cross-country had defeated her sense. She did not care what her next predicament would be — just as long as she no longer had to walk on her aching feet.

"What are you doing, Jade?" Maria asked, and then decided not to bother to wait for an answer. "Oh, what the hell," she acquiesced, because Maria did not care to be left behind alone. The men lifted them into the basket after the balloon had already gone up a couple of feet.

Jade took a deep breath as she lifted her legs over the railing and safely to the base of the basket. She looked up just in time to see the burner flame up to send the envelope of the balloon higher. The burner flamed in a variety of colors, from bright yellow to fiery red, like a rainbow of sizzling colors, but the orange segment sent her eyes bugging, almost freaking her out right there and then. There's something about that color that she just couldn't handle. She couldn't stare at an orange fruit, for instance, without wanting to run for cover. Even peaches frightened her a bit. Had she been in a fire when she was a baby, causing this irrational fear?

Something slapped her in the head and ass. "Wear them for protection," said the little mustached pilot. He looked to see heavy-duty gloves and a long-sleeved dumpy sweatshirt at her feet.

She donned the clothes even though she looked like a petite lumberjack and felt like a stuffed animal. Nevertheless, they did give her the comfort of safety even as the balloon climbed, and the wind escalated.

Burner blaring. Skirt and envelope of the big balloon like a delicate blimp. Basket wobbly when the wind howled but the parachute valve flapping to settle the wind. She felt it all. She experienced exhilaration!

But there was one thing still trying: her feet now felt chilled!

Jade looked down at flatlands, hundreds of feet below her. Only hours earlier she had been driving in a smelly, shitty vehicle. She had been dirty, grimy, and frankly pissed off. Now she loved life. Although she disliked her grubby face, her lumberjack clothes, and especially her cold feet, she could deal with it up in the air where everything was open, expansive, and beautiful.

On the other side of the basket, Bobarino was not feeling her exhilaration. Instead, he was puking over the side of the balloon. Yep, those Italians showed bravado on the outside but were actually wimps. Except that Bobarino's smaller Italian clone captained the balloon expertly, opening up the propane valve just enough to coast upwards at a steady rate.

Meanwhile, George didn't move at all. He was standing exactly in the center of the basket, frozen like an ice sculpture. He gazed straight, eyes level, barely blinking. After watching him perform this balancing act for many minutes, she had to ask: "What are you doing, George?"

"Scared of heights," he managed to whimper. "Didn't realize how bad till now. Thought I could handle this."

"Weren't you gung ho on taking this hot air balloon ride?"

"Yeah," was all he replied.

The last "man" on the boat seemed to feel the opposite of his friend. Kenny jogged a few steps around the outskirts of the basket, patting each corner as he passed. "What are you doing, Kenny?" Jade asked him, not sure if she really wanted to know.

"I'm the Flash!"

Men: how pathetic!

He stopped jogging a moment. "Oh, just kidding," continued Kenny. He must have noticed her incredulous face. "Just getting my juices flowing and keeping warm."

Jade dismissed him then, believing that his first answer was the real one. Instead, she looked for Maria and found her sitting near the propane tanks, gazing fervently at the passing clouds, which seemed more in line with her more quelled exhilaration.

"Can you believe this? Would you have expected a few days ago that we'd be flying through the sky?" Maria asked her.

"It's been wild," Jade replied.

"And may get wilder," the captain said. "Look at those clouds rolling in."

"Figures," both she and Maria said at the same time, not yet coming to the realization of just how dangerous this most recent development could be. Subsequently it dawned on her, busting her exhilarated state. She eyed the threatening clouds before cowering next to Maria at the base of the basket. Meanwhile George remained frozen, Bobarino puked bigger chunks, and Kenny's Flash impersonation quickly changed from a pseudo flash of speed to fearful looks for flashes of lightning.

The winds picked up and the balloon glided in whatever direction the gusts carried it. A drizzle started, drops reaching Jade at a sideways angle, seemingly always finding her eyes before she could blink, which made her tear up like a crying baby.

"Was this in the Jules Verne novel?" Kenny asked.

"Weren't they in Africa or something?" the captain asked.

"Don't you have a balloon to pilot?" Jade implored.

The captain smiled. His stupid mustache creased in such a way that it reminded Jade of an old episode of *Magnum P.I.* if Tom Selleck had turned into a Munchkin with a crooked face.

"This will be fun," the mouth underneath that mustache yelped.

Bobarino's stomach could not be happy.

Kenny glowered at what he thought was a flash of lightning.

Maria coiled where she sat.

George's frozen limbs became colder.

Jade looked at everyone with discomfort and concern.

Chapter 15
Before the Big Day

Freckles had two days before he could execute his plan. He had to wait until Harrison went to town for equipment and could make good on his fishing trip excuse to Lana, who was not privy to their plans, for she would certainly curtail them. Pebbles would be coming along, however.

In the meantime, Freckles didn't know what to do with his time. He couldn't torment the cat because he needed to keep her on his side. Thus, he offered his best behavior around the cat. Likewise, he did not want to antagonize Harrison, either, even though he doubted that the man could be concerned by anyone other than his wife since he was a typical selfish human. Nevertheless, he could not bark, chase squirrels, mind his territory around the house, or jump on any furniture. Also, if he ventured too far beyond their property, he might be tempted to enact part of his plan early, possibly allowing the marten to figure it out. The marten might creep around the house in the next few days, but Freckles had to mind his business and not let the critter get to him, lest it fathom or ruin his plans.

Thus, all he could do was sleep, eat, and sniff familiar objects. *How boring!*

"Oh, husband, dear," Lana said with a sarcastic tone on the second morning of Freckle's boredom. "I am going to do some gardening. If you're going to mow the lawn, please do so away from the garden." The dog believed this comment to be a joke since he'd never seen the old man ever mow the lawn. Usually they hired some kid to do it.

"Oh, so you're daring me to mow the lawn this morning," Harrison yelled back. Of course, he would retort in that way. He often took whatever Lana said as a challenge, but then forgot about it moments later. Since he dismissed the idea that Harrison would mow the lawn, Freckles' boredom would continue. The dog, however, still held hope that Harrison might mow, beyond all expectation, because entertainment would indubitably follow.

The dog lay down then, not tired but unable to think of anything better to do.

Then a small miracle happened. The Rottweiler heard a noise, and not one from the woods. And not the typical yelling between bickering humans, either. Not even the meowing of his new friend, Pebbles. No—instead, he heard the lawn mower come to life.

The sound was quickly followed by hollers: "Oww!" and "My finger!" and "Dammit!" Subsequently, the exciting din of the lawn mower went still.

"What happened, dear?" Lana said, surprisingly without sarcasm.

"Hurt my little pinky on that stupid pulley thing," Harrison replied like a child.

Freckles was unimpressed with the conversation, so remained lying down until the heavenly sound of the mower roared to life once again. He jumped up then. *Boredom averted!*

But the mower died again. "Dammit!"

"Hurt your little pinky again, honey?" the sarcasm coming back into Lana's voice.

"No, just stopped going," the old man said, exasperated. "I've been pulling that pulley thingy again and again, but I can't get it started. And I got to get the lawn mowed before Dara gets here. She won't like the way the lawn looks now."

Lana showed concern then. Freckles knew the look she gave. Her mouth clenched like a bear might as it rummaged through garbage, her eyes tensed like a fox did when it spotted a brave Rottweiler, and her nose twitched like Freckles did when a fly landed on his nose. "Dara's not coming," and then she paused before deciding to continue. "She hasn't been here in years. Since that stupid fight." Freckles waited for the insult that usually accompanied this type of talk with her husband, but it did not come. The concern in her eyes was replaced with a sullen sadness.

"I called her," Harrison said with some seriousness. "That stupid boyfriend is long gone. She told me. She's coming."

"Really—you really called, Harry? Just like that? You swallowed your pride and now all is forgiven?"

Ridicula

"Sometimes you have to do what you have to do to rectify the silliness." Although the words were not profound at all, this might have been the smartest thing Freckles had ever heard Harrison say. Usually, the dog's caretaker was bullheaded, as humans were, but sometimes he could surprise. This surprise had taken two years to happen, but Harrison had finally smartened up.

"Really?" Lana repeated, a question that implied that she didn't believe him. "Well," she transitioned, "the lad that usually does the lawn sometimes presses a button on the side of the mower before starting it. Try that." *No sarcasm. No cruel wit. Odd.*

"Yeah, and Rags is coming, too. I can't wait to wrestle with that Saint Bernard. I remember doing so when I was a lad. Used to tumble around like sticks on charcoal, but neither of us ever got hurt. Lucky, we sure were." Well, Harrison seemed to be going off the deep end again. He seemed to think he was a boy again, at least on some level. *Poor senile old man.*

Lana didn't comment, but a worried expression enveloped her face.

"This new Rags Dara has should be great. Don't know if he's a Saint Bernard, but I can always hope," Harrison continued. Freckles had mixed feelings. He was glad that his caretaker was talking sensibly again, but the Rottweiler wondered if the Rags of years gone by was the only dog Harrison had ever truly cared about.

"Really?" Lana said a third time but did not press her husband after she saw him fumbling with the lawn mower again.

After a minute of mishandling the mower and saying, "No, don't see it" and "Is that the button?" and "Maybe that's it" supplemented with another "Oww!" Freckles knew that things were back to normal. Afterward, he heard the roar of the motor for a third time. This time the din remained.

The dog knew then that more fun would ensue. These humans were nothing if not entertaining in a dimwitted sort of way, even after some intelligence peeked through, so he ran over to Harrison to see what the next commotion would bring.

'You actually are mowing the lawn then?" Lana asked, shouting at her husband even though he seemed to be working for once. "If so, pull some weeds, too. Can you arrange that, Husband?"

"Woman, give me a break!" Harrison yelled just as loudly as his wife. Those humans never stopped bickering for long.

Harrison produced a weed whacker he must have retrieved from the shed so that he could cut the weeds where the mower could not. "It's not you, Wife, who got me to do this. I just need some practice with this thing."

Freckles thought about what the whacky old man was saying. Why would he practice with something he rarely cared to use? Had he decided that caring for the lawn would be his new hobby? That didn't sound like him, though; it involved work.

The dog contemplated longer, still keeping alert for Harrison to come his way with the weed whacker or mower. That old man was liable to accidentally take out an ear. After all, he was currently swinging the whirring weed whacker like a sword.

Then Freckles reasoned why Harrison was operating the weed whacker. He was trying to see whether or not that would be the weapon of choice against the pine marten. Harrison was preparing for the showdown: The Grand Fetcher Escapade: The Ultimate Chase.

Satisfied with this conclusion and proud of Harrison's dedication to defeating the marten, Freckles decided to check up on the cat to see if she was as devoted to the plan as the old man. The dog strode back into the house through the open door. At least one fly followed him inside.

Lana must have seen him because she yelled out, "Hubby, you left the screen ajar again. Shut it before bugs and vermin infest this place." If her words sounded mean-spirited, her tone expressed even more disdain.

Freckles didn't hear Harrison's reply over the delightfully loud purring of the weed whacker. He always had a hankering towards melodic buzzing sounds, and the weed whacker fit that mode. On the other hand, Lana didn't seem so thrilled by it, because she continued, "Just turn that damned thing off for a minute and go close that screen door."

In his doggy manner, Freckles shook his head. Couldn't they stop squabbling just this once? Normally he thought the humans' squabbling to be funny, but not when Harrison was doing something for the dog, so the Rottweiler set his own course of action. With his nose, he pushed at the edge of the screen, propelling it into motion. Carefully he moved the screen shut, only losing his nose grip once during the feat.

Meanwhile, the weed whacker remained purring. Harrison had no intention of shutting it down. Moments later, Lana stormed into the kitchen ready to scream some more, when she saw that the screen was shut thanks to the Rottweiler. Perplexed but calming, she moved on. Thus, for the moment, the bickering stopped, to Freckle's relief.

He trotted on to find the cat. Where was that kitty? Didn't she know that she didn't need to hide now that they were on this temporary truce? Freckles shrugged, doggy shoulders aloft, no longer wanting to guess at the thoughts of felines.

Then, suddenly, Pebbles jumped on top of him from underneath the blanket hanging above the crown of the couch. To say that Freckles was startled was an understatement. Never before had any animal, let alone a cat, attacked him. He yelped in response, louder as the cat's claws dug into him. What had gotten into this fiendish feline?

Not much caring about the answer, only wishing the pain away, the dog shook the cat off. Pebbles flew across the room and into a wall. Luckily her cat reflexes allowed her to bounce off the wall with her bottom, do a somersault in the air, and land on the floor on her feet. She didn't stop with that, either, immediately running like a train, claw tracks in the rug.

Freckles stared disbelievingly as Pebbles nearly smashed into the opposite wall, narrowly missing it in favor of the hallway. The cat zigzagged down the hallway like a snake playing with a slinky. Afterward, she disappeared through the bedroom door and underneath the humans' bed.

The dog went to investigate the blanket from where the cat had leapt, and the mystery of the crazy cat was solved. Lying beside the blanket was a scrunched up hairball laced with catnip. Pebbles must have been testing the catnip in preparation for tomorrow's big face-off with the marten.

Freckles grinned. His accomplices were taking his plan seriously. They would be ready. He certainly would be, too.

Chapter 16
The Ranger

He knew it was inevitable.
Without fail he always ended up here—and usually driving on this very road. And it wasn't like they were traveling down a big highway, like 80 or 90 or even 25. No, it was RT 20 that summoned him, whether entering from the Idaho or Nebraska side.

So, with a mix of emotions, Hippie stared at *the* sign, which he had seen so many times: *WELCOME TO WYOMING*.

Now, if he happened to like traveling this way, perhaps to explore the woodsy vitality of Yellowstone Park, he wouldn't mind. But he had explored Yellowstone on many occasions (as well as all the rest of Wyoming). He would rather be elsewhere—even New Jersey!

Plus, besides the obvious inevitability of it, he hadn't known that Maude was heading here, at least until the landscapes of Idaho became familiar. Yes, potato fields could become distinguishable after seeing them so much.

Yet, for all its tediousness, Hippie still enjoyed Wyoming. After all, he knew many of the restaurants, for he had been hired to cook for many dives and pubs of Wyoming. During his drifting and working, he had encountered many fine Wyomians, from lumberjacks to dishwashers, from hillbillies to rangers, from grease monkeys to musicians—all unique, mostly friendly, and rarely disingenuous.

Still, Maude would not disclose the full reason for them coming here, although he was certain that it had to do with the somewhat guiltless but still illegal activities at Lake Tahoe. And surprisingly, neither Carolyn nor Jim (who still followed them in his pickup) seemed to mind making this trip. He didn't know why. Didn't they have a life to go home to? Yet, he didn't want to pry too deeply into their purposes for coming. Although he suspected their motives, he would let it play out as it may.

Maude suddenly pulled the 4X4 over to the side, caroming off the road like a pigeon attempting to escape from a New York City cab. "Okay, lady, here's where you get off."

"What the fuck?" Carolyn replied, tone and blasphemy sounding like Maude. Until now, Carolyn hadn't participated in all the cursing that Hippie and Maude had done during the many hours on the road. She mostly had kept quiet, agreeing or adding a harmless declaration about a topic here or a comment there. After all, she hadn't much interest in jerky or niacin or baseball so had little to contribute. And because of this, she and Maude had mostly gotten along in recent hours. Thus, throwing her out now seemed arbitrary even for Maude.

"Yep, time to go," Maude continued, not angry, just matter-of-fact.

Bearman's pickup drew to a halt behind Maude's truck, parked only three quarters off the road. Other drivers slowed down to honk as they passed, but Jim paid them no mind; he could care less about any honks, unless they sounded gospel or angelic.

To Hippie's extreme surprise, Carolyn exited the car without so much as one syllable of added disputation. Instead, she addressed Hippie. "If you see George, send him my regards." This might have been the sanest remark she had spoken since joining them, because it meant that her obsession with finding George had finally diminished—maybe.

A while had passed since Carolyn had mentioned George; so much time in fact that Hippie had temporally forgotten about her real purpose for staying with them for so long. For some odd reason, she had thought that they would run into George at some point in their travels. Hippie guessed that she had finally given up on the notion once they entered the great state of Wyoming. Who finds anybody they know by chance in Wyoming? He had never done so in all his travels to the marvelous state.

But then, why had Carolyn embarked on this venture? She must have known that they would wind up in Wyoming sooner rather than later. After all, Hippie was still Hippie, and Hippie ALWAYS ventured to Wyoming.

These thoughts about Carolyn gnawed at his inner being. Thus, understandably, he was reminded that he was due for another dose of niacin.

Carolyn walked toward Bearman's pickup, and Jim opened the door in gentlemanly manner: exiting his truck, honkers be damned, and opening the passenger's side for her. She plopped herself on the seat without a word.

"Are you sure about this, Maude?" Hippie asked. "She barely knows that man, and he may be all Jesus-loving on the surface, but who knows what he's really like."

"I have a feelin' Carolyn can take care of herself," Maude replied. "He'd take a heavy knee to his groin if he were to act up. Anyway, I think he's the real deal, unlike those lowlifes he hung out with. Not sure about Carolyn, though. She may or may not be a reporter, but she is certainly neurotic, wants her way, and is a liar. I guess that's reporting nowadays."

Hippie chuckled at her cynicism but did not feel the same way. Sure, outlandish and maniacal reporting occurred, but most news people were just trying to seek the truth in an unfair, Trumpian society. As for Carolyn, he realized that he still knew little about her. Was she really who she said she was? He doubted it, but he didn't let the question linger. That's because he didn't much care about the answer, as this was his trusting nature.

If Maude thought that Bearman would turn around and take Carolyn home, she was as misguided as a model without a mirror, except that Maude had no use for a mirror and would probably crack it if she had one. Unsurprisingly then, when Maude put the pedal to the metal, Jim's pickup followed right along. "Don't they realize that kicking out Carolyn was my way of saying I no longer wanted either of them following us?" Maude asked, exasperated.

"Of course not," Hippie replied.

"Do you know why they are here in the first place?" Maude asked, chagrined.

"Not really."

"Do you care?"

"Nah." He would find out when the time came. Nature would tell him at the right moment. No need to worry about it.

"They want to ruin my whole operation," Maude went on, trying to tell Hippie what he didn't need to know. "They're not confiscating my peyote emeralds and entire petrified logging line."

"Peyote emeralds?" Hippie asked, not curious but interested nonetheless.

"You know, one of my precious minerals I mentioned."

"Oh," he said, seemingly not caring whether she elaborated or not. Smoking peyote of any kind wasn't his thing. But smoking an emerald might be cool. The beryl minerals might produce some interesting flavor.

"That reporter is gonna ruin everything. Why did I bring her this far?"

"'Cause you know she's not really a reporter," Hippie replied, stating what he found obvious.

"But what if she really is?" Maude looked nervous, which was unlike her, and her fear was completely unfounded.

"What if I'm really Jesus?" Hippie gave her his whimsical smile.

"Bearman would love that, wouldn't he?" she asked in reply with her quick, guttural chuckle.

Now miles into Wyoming and putting his mixed feelings about the state aside, Hippie decided to enjoy the scenery of Yellowstone Park. No matter how many times he had come or would go, the beauty of the park heightened his senses and gave him a high that no peyote could. That would always be the case for him unless climate change ruined his natural high.

Hippie opened the window to feel the breeze on his hands. Then he extended his head out as a large dog might. While his hand did not feel the temperature immediately, his head bore the chilly gust with a teary vehemence. He persevered, keeping his head out the window, continuing to bear the fresh piercing cold but wondering how he could be enjoying the icy air when, not long ago, his alter ego had been waterskiing with a warm breeze blowing into him.

Through his teary eyes he recognized a beautiful larch, which had branches protruding onto the road, from which he could see a few leaves fall even though it was only late August. He loved larches, because it was one of the few deciduous conifers and a beauty in nature. This one was particularly stunning with its enormous height, its prickly pine fragrance, and an elegance that seemed to emanate throughout the woodlands; thus, he made a point to acknowledge it every time he passed it, which was often enough. "Oh, larch tree, show me your beauty, and let me hear your allure." In response, the tree seemed to call out its quick melodic tune in the breeze.

"What are you yapping about now?" asked Maude, used to his affinity with nature but still letting it be known that she found it odd, especially when he talked aloud to trees and such.

"Behold the larch," he responded in jest, although they had sped by it already.

"Lovely," she said dismissively. "Are those clowns still behind us?"

He had temporarily forgotten all about Carolyn and Bearman. He twisted his head against the wind and could barely see the truck through his tears even though it was still pretty close. "Yep."

"Foolish fucking fools," she announced, stressing "fool" twice as she put metal to the truck pedal.

"You have a real truck. Jim has a pickup. You really think you can outgun him?" he asked, finally returning his head fully into the truck, tears from the wind streaming down both cheeks.

"Nah, but I bet a pickup can't go through trees!" Maude replied, veering off the road into a forest that was likely protected under federal law. Hippie didn't care much about that law, but he did care about getting his handsome face gnarled against a big beefy tree.

Maude did not hit the tree head-on. Instead, she sideswiped it and the next and the next on both sides until the truck entered a clearing, which Hippie had not seen from the roadway. It seemed that Bearman had also not seen the clearing so had chosen not to follow.

With minimal damage to her truck, and thankfully, to the trees as well, Maude came to a stop. "Let's go before those two nincompoops spot us and follow on foot." She opened the door and jumped out, running when she touched ground. She was extremely limber for such a broad woman, so much so that Hippie did not think he could achieve such a feat. He opened the door more carefully and stepped out.

"Come on, you sissy," Maude yammered, running to where the woods grew thick again. "Let's go."

Hippie obliged, caught up in this whole escape concoction that Maude had fabricated. He didn't have any reason to believe that Carolyn and Jim had any other reason for coming other than just to be tagging along in Bearman's case and hoping somehow to run into George Cramwell in Carolyn's case. Hippie could not imagine George being a suspect in anything, let alone in a crime as important enough to make any news, fake or not. George could be a buffoon at times, but he was honorable and would never commit a felony, at least not since he'd stopped his crime spree in his youth.

"You're lucky those other two clowns haven't found the truck yet," Maude said when Hippie finally caught up to her. "I would have had to leave you to your own devices. And you'd try to befriend a wolf and offer it flowers, surely getting yourself ripped apart and eaten."

"Okay, Maude," he responded, attempting to roll his eyes, acting like he wouldn't do as she said but knowing that he would. "They're not trying to find us anyway."

Then, before he could finish, he heard Carolyn's voice. "There's the truck. I told you they didn't really crash."

Maude scolded him with her eyes; they stated that he was the dumbest, most naïve fool this side of the Rocky Mountains. Without a word, she moved on through the coppice.

Hippie thought of finding the other two instead of continuing to follow Maude. But then he would be leaving nature in favor of people. That was certainly not him, so instead he decided to pursue a bird's call, which happened to be singing in the direction that Maude had taken. This way, nature guided him instead of the broad-shouldered whacky woman.

When he could not hear the bird any longer, he searched for anything that would help determine where he should move next. He settled on a scurrying rabbit he spotted ahead, which perchance, was following the trail that Maude had left behind. When the rabbit veered out of his sight, he felt for the wind to guide him on and moved with tranquility, listening for the wind's music in the rustling of leaves. In this way, he moved always in Maude's direction but never catching her. Occasionally he saw the woman glance back, usually with disgust, but he barely heeded her.

They continued like this for what seemed hours until finally the wind died down enough for him to hear Maude calling him. "Hey, nitwit. Get your head together. We're almost there."

Climbing out of the clouds in his head, he found his words. "I still don't know where we're going."

"Now that I think we lost your demented bear and that other demonic friend of yours, you'll be finding out shortly," Maude coughed out, which finally broke his prolonged peace in nature.

Hippie caught Maude as she rounded a spruce. "Are you meeting with your buddies again like you did in Tahoe?"

"Nah, just retrieving some goodies, including some peyote emeralds. A girl has got to make her truck payment, you know."

"What about your petrified logging? Doesn't that pay for something?" Hippie asked, starting not to care even as he asked the question.

"Ah, yes, that will make some dough. But it's all for the children. We are a charity after all. Remember?"

"Oh yeah. KIDS." Hippie had totally forgotten until that instant, but this forgetfulness made him realize that he had to re-energize his mind and cleanse his body again. He popped a niacin pill into his mouth. One should do for now. No sense in becoming too ruddy. With two, his appearance might clash with the piney terrain, but a healthy one-pill hue would work just fine.

They continued onward or in a circle or square pattern; for all their walking, they seemed not to be getting very far. Hippie swore he had just seen the red grapevine they now passed twenty minutes ago, but he took it all in stride. He was in no rush.

He stared longingly. Although he was no expert in identifying types of grapes, these made his mouth water for cabernet sauvignon red wine. And maybe one more pill of niacin, which might not make his face clash as much as he thought it might just a moment ago.

Then the wild grapevine lay behind him, hopefully for good this time. He had no Cab to drink anyway.

"Did you bring any beer in that backpack?" he asked Maude, just now noticing that she wore one.

She reached in, grabbed a beer, and tossed it to him. She produced another for herself. This stuff was not exactly Cab, but it would counter the niacin pill nicely.

They walked through a copse and around a large evergreen. There, in a clearing that let in rays of sunlight from every direction, either directly or by reflection rays, Hippie saw something that could forever change his life.

Or at least make him very happy.

He saw a garden.

But not any garden. Here, mounds and mounds of mushrooms grew, mostly portabellas, on a raised bed with neighboring green peas and asparagus, a barely visible tap root that could only mean one type of food: sunflower seeds and dirt pots filled with nearly ripe avocados. Beyond them, he saw bell peppers and broccoli stalks growing from deep soil. This odd assortment of vegetables were all rich with B3.

Yes, he had stumbled upon a niacin garden!

Sure, chicken and pork had an abundance of niacin, but for vegetables these were the shit. Especially the mushrooms which lay in compost of manure.

"Have you reached heaven yet?" Maude asked with a large grin, which looked out of place on her often-austere face.

"You knew this garden of niacin heaven was here?" Hippie asked back to her, his excitement barely contained. He wanted to charge into the garden and eat everything. In late summer, the vegetables were ready for harvesting. Perfect timing!

'Yeah; my ranger buddy plants them. He loves his niacin as much as you do. Probably put pork on the grill if you'd like, too."

Only then did he see the cabin behind the garden. This had to be the ranger's home or headquarters, although it didn't seem like much of a place to work or live. It looked smaller than a shed. More like a kid's clubhouse, really.

Then, someone walked out of the cabin. He thought it would be the ranger, but it was only a boy. He couldn't be more than fifteen years old, barely able to shave and smaller than most boys that age, too. He was extremely pale, as if he had not been in the sun in a very long time. Yet, his golden hair glimmered, and his bloodshot eyes radiated embers in the sun, a peculiar guise for any kid.

"Maude, Maude, what a pleasure," the boy greeted with a surprising husky voice.

"Likewise," replied Maude in a deep voice that somehow seemed less husky than the boy. "This is Aspen," she continued. "A fellow niacin lover."

"This is the ranger?" asked Hippie.

"My ranger, yes," responded Maude.

"I oversee her lands," said the kid.

"You own a part of Yellowstone Park?" Hippie asked, incredulous.

"Oh, poor Aspen, always confused," Maude replied, electing to use his real name to emphasis his innocence. "Of course, I don't own it. That don't mean I don't use it. I have my stuff all over this park but mostly in the cabin, which my ranger protects." She guzzled the last part of her beer down and threw it on the ground. Then she flattened the can with one big stomp.

"Protects? How?"

The kid answered by performing a wheelhouse kick followed by five quick chops in the air. Then he flipped like an acrobatic monkey, landing at Hippie's side in position to strike like a cornered snake.

"Oh, I see," Hippie said, impressed. Where did this kid learn such skills? But as was his way, he did not bother to ask. His curiosity had already dissipated. Instead, he asked, "And you were willing to show me this location to me? You trust me that much?"

"Well, why not? You are a trustworthy hippy, and some think you are Jesus, too." She laughed her gruff laugh. The boy followed suit with a laugh gruffer than hers. *Go figure.*

"So, what is it that you want, Maude?" the pale but gruff voiced karate champ asked.

"Some peyote emeralds, of course. Ah, hell, how about all of them?"

"As you wish."

They walked to the clubhouse and the kid threw open the door. Hippie peered in—and his mouth dropped.

What he saw was beyond anything he could have imagined.

Chapter 17
Bloodshedder

The balloon spiraled out of control.

At least that's what Kenny thought when the wind smashed into him.

He held on for dear life. He felt that the wind from the storm was going to push him overboard. He could read the headlines: *Idiot Thirty-One-Year-Old Scmuck Splatters atop Yellowstone Geyser*. Those paparazzi don't care about human lives—just the outrageous story.

"Get down, you idiot!" yelled Jade. She must have paparazzi blood in her.

He did as he was told, explaining, "I just wanted to see the geyser."

"In case you haven't noticed, there's still a storm out there!" screamed Jade over the hollowing wind.

"I couldn't tell, because my stomach was trying to puke out anything left of my intestines." Kenny touched his stomach and felt the rumbling. He hadn't eaten in what felt like a millenium. "How long have we been up here? Why haven't we landed to wait out the storm?"

The mustached pilot semi-twin of Bobarino heard him. "Haven't you been listening to me? It's safer to wait out the storm from the air. Landing would be too dangerous. But the storm has lasted a long time. We must descend soon anyway."

"So, we are going to land during the storm? We've drifted all the way into Wyoming, or Oz, or wherever Hell is, just to die?" Maybe Kenny was being dramatic, but he was more than a little pissed off, cranky, and ready to raise hell.

"The storm is letting up. See the sun peeking out from the clouds slightly eastward?" responded the pilot. At first, Kenny had no idea where to look because the sun was mostly hidden by dark menacing clouds. He turned his head all around like a spaz on amphetamines and finally glimpsed a patch of sun, realizing at the same moment that the rain was letting up, only soaking his sodden body instead of entirely drenching it.

Swearing never to ride a hot air balloon again in this lifetime, Kenny tried to remain patient as he groped the bottom of the gondola. He didn't think he'd try again to stand up until they were safely on the ground. Even from his limited vantage point, he could see the pilot manipulating some gear and then felt the balloon lighten and begin its descent.

"I think I see a slight clearing in the woods, and the rain has let off enough for us to land," the pilot said shakily, giving Kenny little confidence.

"Are you sure this is a good place to land?" Maria asked, echoing Kenny's thoughts.

"As good as any, especially since we are so low on fuel," replied the pilot.

Ah, no fuel. Sounds right, Kenny thought, his hands trembling ever so slightly as he imagined plummeting into the trees. But at least there would be less of a chance of the balloon exploding due to an empty gas tank. That was Kenny—always the optimist!

In other words, he was certain that the outcome would be a fiery death.

The air balloon drifted downward quickly. The plummet was beginning. His feet joined his hands with the quivering sensation.

Maria knelt beside him. "Why are you men such wimps? Bobarino looks like he's about to have a heart attack, but at least he stopped puking and panicking. George is frozen with fear. And you, forget about it," she said like one of Tony Soprano's goons might. "We're through the storm. Why don't you try again to get those shaky legs to stand up?"

"I'm fine right here," he replied. "I'll wait until we've landed."

"No, you're going to help us land," Maria ordered. Kenny thought she was Jade for a moment; Jade did the commanding, not Maria.

"Oh, my poor feet," he heard Jade moan for the millionth time. For some reason, that gave him strength. He did not want to be so pathetic. He really didn't.

But a little more encouragement was necessary.

Maria must have seen his uncertainty about what he should do next. He guessed that was pretty obvious by the way he still cowered on the floor. "Get up, you good for nothing fool!" *What had gotten into her?*

Kenny decided to at least lift himself to his knees. *That showed some bravery, right?*

"You are such a coward!" exclaimed Maria and kicked him lightly in the shin. "Mice are braver than you."

Okay, that was enough. He leapt to his feet and found that he could stand without the wind knocking him off the railing. That was a relief. The wind had died down a great deal, but he said, "I'm much taller than you, Maria, so I'm much more likely to lose my balance." *Even wimps had to defend themselves sometimes.*

"Oh, so you're calling me short now," she yelled over the wind, but she laughed before he could take her seriously. "Standing wasn't THAT hard, was it?"

"I almost did fall before. I could have already been ant meat by now," he pleaded, another weak attempt to justify his cowardly actions.

Then the pilot interrupted. "You better all lay low. Navigating these trees may be difficult."

Kenny quickly sat down again. "Back down after all that effort," he jibed.

"And you sit so well," Maria jibed back. The others joined them in the lower echelons of the basket, huddling together as if calling a play in a football game. George ruined that image for Kenny because he plopped down in the middle of them all and stared up at nothing in particular like a paralyzed zombie unable to rise from the dead.

Jade looked at him with disgust. "Just pathetic."

"Right on," Maria added.

George seemed always to be the disparaged one no matter what he did. Kenny had to admit that his friend wasn't helping his cause now. George hadn't reacted to anything said about him during most of the hot air balloon voyage and remained silent now.

Kenny decided to speak out for George. "Why don't you just leave him alone?"

"He got us in this mess," replied Jade. "He's such a putz."

"He never dragged us anywhere. We're responsible, too." And then, at the oddest moment he ever could have imagined, as the balloon descended and the wind picked up once more, he asked Jade, "Whatever happened to you two anyway? You used to actually care for each other." With these words, he felt courageous for the first time in a long while. He had always been afraid to ask, because it seemed they both wanted it that way, but he just had to find out the scandalous details sometime. It might as well be right before he died.

"Now you finally become brave," Maria said, echoing Kenny's thoughts. She had a knack for that—almost a kindred sense.

"What the heck? We're all going to be dead in a few moments anyway." Kenny laughed, but Maria responded by smacking him in the face, not at all amused but not offended, either.

The pilot took that moment to speak up. "We're in for a bumpy landing—if we can avoid the trees, that is."

In other words, they were smashing into the trees for their untimely and excruciating deaths. But somehow, this thought gave him more bravado, and he asked again, "What the hell happened to you two?"

Jade grimaced at him. George stared at nothing. It looked like he wasn't going to get his answer.

Then Jade suddenly yelled, "He cheated on me, all right?" That was the last thing he would have expected. She cheating on him, sure, but not the other way around.

"Bloodshedder!" George screamed, possibly the first word he said since the storm encroached. *Insanity aside, George has spoken!*

Kenny immediately rethought his optimism, because George then spouted nonsense as if acting in a dizzying one-camera slasher movie. "Bloodshedder will get me! Bloodshedder will take my blood and soul! Bloodshedder will harvest my intestines! Bloodshedder! Bloodshedder!" *What or who the fuck was "Bloodshedder" anyway?*

He could not readily ask George's meaning for two reasons: 1) George stared into oblivion, not appearing to have the intellectual capability to elaborate or even say another word, and 2) The balloon was about to smash into a tree.

"Fore!" the captain yelled with no sense. First off, they were not mishitting a ball in golf, unless the balloon was the ball. Secondly, who was he telling to watch out: the tree?

Kenny had known it all along; they were doomed.

In golf, when the ball is hit correctly with a driver, the ball's flight reaches its pinnacle in the air before arcing downward to the fairway. Luckily or perhaps due to some skill of the pilot, the air balloon acted like a golf ball and dipped below a branch of the tree just in time.

Or nearly so, anyway.

The tip of the envelope of the balloon grazed the branch, but all seemed well when the balloon continued to drift down steadily—

Until it didn't.

The balloon plummeted faster as the scratch in the envelope became a hole. There went the perfect flight of the golf ball, spiraling down into the rough or worse.

Kenny resumed his thoughts of doom.

Everyone screamed in terror, including the pilot. All except George, that is. He made no sound, calm as could be, only watching the balloon deflate like a tire on a spike.

Was "Bloodshedder" a premonition? Was the air balloon the "Bloodshedder" he had referenced? Would all of them be bleeding as they were horribly ripped to shreds? But then the name would have been "Bloodshredder"!

Kenny dared to look down, seeing another smaller tree directly below the basket. Before he could scream louder, the basket bounced off the tree like a beach ball in the sand. For an instant, they flew upwards. Then, gravity took hold, and they continued to plummet.

Except they didn't. Instead, the basket bounced off another tree, the friction causing the balloon to slow. Hitting the ground, the basket bounced once, then again and one more time until settling on its side a few meters from the previous spot.

As the basket flipped, so did Kenny. He slammed hard to the ground, stunned but otherwise uninjured.

Had they all miraculously escaped unharmed?

The envelope of the air balloon deflated and tumbled around them, narrowly missing Kenny as he crawled to safety. Rain patted his head and dirt smeared his face before he realized that it might be better to lift his head as he crawled. He dragged his legs, though. His pants ripped, causing him to yell out, "Damn it!" even though that should have been the last of his worries.

"Are you all right?" he heard the pilot ask in a squeaky voice, as if he had suddenly turned into a talking mouse.

Kenny turned his face toward the noise and found that the pilot was not talking to him; he was talking to Bobarino, who was facedown and unmoving in the dirt. The pilot shook him, but Bobarino did not respond.

"I'll get help, I will," the pilot squealed. Then he ran off crazily, raising his arms and yelling "Help!" as he dashed out of sight. Kenny didn't think to stop him. He was too busy spitting out dirt.

His legs too wobbly to stand, Kenny managed to crawl to Bobarino's side. He shook him and then turned him over on his back. The effort was clumsy, but he still felt he had done it close to what he'd learned in CPR class about a dozen years ago. (He had just finished two years of college, and having little direction in life, had become gung-ho about joining the Peace Corps, based on a TV ad. That excitement had lasted all of two weeks, but that had been enough time for him to sign up and take the Red Cross class.)

This extensive two-week experience allowed him to tell that Bobarino was still breathing and that nothing was blocking his throat passage, or whatever the doctors called it. Then he was able to deduce that the Italian man was unconscious. After all, he still wasn't moving.

That's where Kenny's recollection of CPR class ended. He looked around for the others. Maybe they would know better what to do.

But he didn't see anyone.

What happened to them? Had they been thrown from the balloon like ragdolls? Were they all lying in a ditch, unconscious, too? Were they dead?

His unfounded fears subsided when he saw Maria walk into view, unhurt, unbloodied, her hair only slightly disheveled, and lovely.

Behind her, Jade looked annoyed but was also uninjured. Her hair lay perfectly in place, but that did not appeal to him. And she wore no shoes once more, for her most recent pair must have gone flying off in the wind.

At that moment, Bobarino jumped to his feet. "Blimey," he said, a rather unusual word coming from an Italian.

"Are you all right?" Kenny asked, concern arising more from Bobarino speaking British than because he had just been unconscious.

"Bloody good," replied the Italian, and he didn't seem at all sarcastic.

What the hell? Kenny thought but decided not to inquire further about the other's condition. *If he says he's all right, then he's all right.*

"Where's Waldo—I mean, George?" Jade asked, and then added, "Missing again. What a dimwit!"

"Maybe he's finally gone to get you those perfect glass slippers," Kenny answered but instantly regretted it as Jade smacked him.

"Perhaps he went to get help, like the pilot did?" asked Maria.

"No, he's not smart enough," Jade replied.

"Maybe he's lost, hurt, or dead," Kenny avowed, echoing his glum mood.

"No, I'm not lucky enough," Jade responded, but she wasn't fooling him. She had asked about his whereabouts with a little concern in her mocking.

"Well, he didn't just disappear," Maria declared.

"He did with that woman." Jade professed. There it was. The crux of it all said at last. "And he acted all innocent when he finally did return. But I knew better."

"Let's just find him," Kenny suggested, perhaps the first sensible thing he had said this entire trip.

They searched through the balloon wreck and nearby bushes, trees, ditch, and dirt. They couldn't find any footprint, ripped clothing, or any other sign of him. George was simply missing.

Perhaps he had vanished after all.

Chapter 18
The Dawn of Reckoning

The old man could be infuriating, Freckles thought. *Don't humans know that starting battery-charged weed whackers in the forest could alarm other animals, including our marten target? Man-made crap always concerned the animal denizens. That's why Harrison wasn't supposed to start the whacker till later. So what if the old man had a few thorns prickling him? Just stop clearing stuff out whenever a thorn threatens your fragile piece of skin. Take the prick, old man!*

It's dawn, too, with patches of darkness still lurking. He probably can't see. He'll injure himself with that whacker.

Meanwhile, the demented cat was enthralled with her catnip, running around the forest like a crazy chipmunk, scratching every leaf and stick she could find. Well, at least the marten wouldn't suspect the noise to be something which should concern him. After all, what predator would announce themselves with such noise? Perhaps a stupid human. That's why Harrison infuriated the Rottweiler so much—not so much the noise, just the foolishness.

Since Freckles was a rather large dog, he couldn't sneak through the forest all that quietly either, so perhaps all this racket might be for the best. Deception might prove more valuable than all-out surprise. At least he hoped so.

Although he was always confident of success, Freckles knew that his new archenemy was both smart and wily and had made a fool of him in the past. Now, he would get the best of the marten at that same location: The Douglas-fir tree, the Grand Fetcher, where the ultimate chase was bound to go. His archenemy would be trapped and begging for Freckles' clemency.

If his accomplices didn't bungle things up.

They moved onward. The marten would be appearing near the tree when the sun rose just above the Grand Fetcher. Freckles had noticed that pattern from the marten while scouting out this location in preparation for this glorious day. No matter what he was doing:

chasing prey, sleeping, or causing havoc, the marten always went to the Douglas-fir tree. That's why he had decided to have the marten come to the trap, rather than Freckles seek his archenemy out. That just made sense.

Not like those humans, Freckles thought while dropping his ears to avoid listening to Harrison's weed whacker. *Their wars, inclinations, and logic were "Ridicula,"* which in Freckles' vernacular meant: *well beyond ridiculous, approaching stupidity and insanity; mostly associated with humans.*

Since the marten already knew or would learn immediately after arriving that they were in the vicinity, Freckles had to trick the marten by exposing his biggest weakness: his bravado. That little weasel thought he was smarter and faster than any of them, and he might be right about that. After all, the cat continued to act like a possessed bouncy ball while the human was, well, human. But the marten would consider this ragtag team incapable, and thus his overconfidence could be his undoing. Therefore, the element of surprise via sneaking wasn't needed; Freckles had other surprises waiting for the dastardly marten.

The Grand Fetcher was in plain sight now and they didn't need to move closer, so finally Harrison stopped that confounded weed-whacker, for he had no more weeds or brush to clear. Now, the primary purpose of bringing the weed whacker would be employed, if Harrison understood what he was to do. *A big if. Ridicula!*

As for that cat, acting crazy on catnip suited Freckles' plans, although he hoped Pebbles hadn't expended it all already. The cat loved catnip!

But now, they waited.

After two minutes, Harrison said, "How long must we wait?" *Impatient human.*

Freckles did not have the proper vocal appartus to answer in a way that the man would understand quickly, so the dog did nothing in response.

"Just don't ruin my plan," said Harrison. *His plan. Yeah, right!* Freckles laughed uproariously in his thoughts but just kept it to himself. Let him think what he wanted, as long as he played his role.

They continued to wait. After five more minutes, Harrison said, "This is ridiculous. That marten ain't coming. I'm going home."

Freckles knew that Harrison could be impatient but had not anticipated him to be this hasty. After all, Harrison could fish all day and catch nothing. He just waited there with a fishing rod. Wasn't this waiting business much the same? It's not like he splashed around the lake scaring all the fish when they did not bite, like Freckles would have done. The guy just didn't know how to have a good time.

Then, Freckles heard a familiar sound of rustling. The marten was close. Now the fun would begin.

The marten popped out of a bush that Harrison had just weed-whacked, scaring Pebbles half to death, causing her to jump out of her fur and twirling in the air like ballerina on catnip. In return, the marten gave them all his sardonic smile.

"Damn nuisance," Harrison said, starting back up his weed whacker. "You're asking for it now."

The marten cackled, not at all fearful of the bumbling man. So instead of retreating, the marten advanced on the man, probably trying to trip up the old man for another good laugh.

Luckily, this action was exactly what Freckles had expected the marten to do. Harrison, however, was surprised, almost dropping the weed whacker when the marten ran right over the man's foot. Pebbles, meanwhile had landed on her feet, but the marten tripped her up when he zigzagged by, taking out her front paws.

Not exactly as Freckles intended, but it would do.

Freckles reacted, running after the marten like a dog after a mailman. The chase was on again.

But this time, the dog was more controlled and more prepared. Ready for this particular chase. Ready to win.

Rascally Rascal saw his chance to be mischievous again. This dog, Freckles, and his ragtag team didn't know when to call it quits. Let's see. Who should he pick on first? The inept old man, the scaredy-cat, or the mulish dog? He thought about it for only second, and then had his answer; he'd pick on all three.

Frightening the cat was easy. All he had to do was show his face, for that cat was on something, jumping around like a crazed bunny. And the old man's reaction was priceless, starting up his cutting-hedge contraption. *Did he think he was going to scare me with that thing? Ha!*

As expected, the dogged dog gave chase after MOOC embarrassed the others. He scrambled away, thinking of the best way to get the dog trapped in the tree again. That would be hilarious! And the Rottweiler deserved it, too, for the dog never gave up. *Somewhat admirable,* MOOC admitted. *But he needed to be given a lesson.*

That Freckles character would never catch Rascally Rascal. That was obvious, probably even to that dimwitted loco cat, but the dog bashed his way through branches and bushes, on and on after Nocturnal Nuisance anyway. Eventually, when he tired the dog out sufficiently, the marten would loop back to the Douglas-fir and let the entanglement happen. MOOC wondered just how long it would take him to escape this time. He chuckled outwardly, making sure that the dog noticed.

It was time. That dog looked exhausted. The marten ran to the tree, darting under it like he had done before. The dog would scramble after him and get himself trapped; if not right away, the marten would duck and dance enough so that the dog would become entangled. After all, MOOC knew the insides and outs of this tree. It was one of his favorite eating spots, after all.

Then he saw the cat who, for some reason, still danced crazily around the tree. Perhaps Rascally Rascal could trap the dumb cat, too. He changed his direction ever so slightly to go after the cat. As he did so, the hummingbirds emerged out of nowhere. How could he have not sensed them? He must have been so focused on the chase that he had ignored his surroundings. He felt ashamed. *Rookie mistake!*

The tiny hummingbirds, which MOOC counted at seven, swooped to him, humming like honeybees as they approached. Before he could react, they were upon him, confounding and misdirecting. And the cat was no help, still leaping around like a clawed lunatic frog, barely seeing possible prey in the hummingbirds. The kitty just added to MOOC's bewilderment.

With all this hubbub, the marten scrambled underneath the tree, and before he could orient himself, one of his claws struck a twig which seemed out of place, for he knew every nook and cranny of the Grand Fetcher. A part of him realized what that meant. MOOC had pulled a trick like this in a different part of the woods many times. But these three couldn't be clever enough to achieve this feat. He slowed anyway.

Too late. The box dropped, covering him entirely. Rascally Rascal had been trapped by one of his own ruses.

Chapter 19
The Rich and the Obsessed

Hippie breathed heavily, trying to take it all in. For such a confined space, there was an awful lot to see.

At the forefront of the quaint establishment lay a table that must have been constructed when the Amish way of life was the norm. It was finely crafted, almost like the wood had been stitched with the use of a sewing machine. Every roundlet detail was carved and woven like a spiraling staircase leading to the mahogany balcony, which exhibited artwork that the likes of Cézanne and Van Gogh would have difficulty replicating. The surface, exquisite in texture and style, depicted flowery and fruity imagery that looked like still-life wood sculpture. The chairs masterfully accompanied the table. Although unlikely to be part of the same set, the chairs had the same type of craftsmanship, interwoven in detail and unmatched by the machines which made today's furniture. Hippie dared not sit on one of the chairs, not to chance breaking it, for they looked sturdy enough, but for fear of ruining its disposition ever so slightly.

Nothing stood on the table save a single emerald. Surely this was one of the peyote emeralds in which Maude was so enamored. Now he knew why. This one's green effervescence sparkled like nothing he had ever seen, emitting a smoky light that could break down the fog on a gloomy day or the smog in LA. Other emeralds of the same nature radiated off the walls with such splendor that even the greatest of fireworks displays could not render such magnificence. Each of the emeralds seemed to be linked in perfect synchronicity with their leader, the table's lone object.

While the sculpted table, chairs, and emeralds showcased the place, there was so much more the clubhouse had to offer. Every nook and cranny held artwork: paintings, watercolors, posters, and wrappers, or natural beauty, such as petrified leaves, prism-like crystals, naturally sculpted bark, and cherry blossoms. And the walls depicted more drawings, texts in many different languages, and ancient scrolls whose parchment was barely strung together. Christmas clothes similar to those of which he had seen earlier in the week littered much of the floor space. Hippie realized that it could take days or weeks to explore every detail of the interior of this eight square-foot wooden marvel.

Hippie looked around some more—this time taking in the clubhouse architecture. It seemed like nothing special, but there was something about the craftmanship that intrigued him. After another second, he realized what it was. "This place is made of the nearby petrified wood forest, correct? "

"You got it, bro," replied Maude and then addressed the boy, "Now get to work, Ranger! I've got some money to make."

The ranger boy got busy collecting emeralds for Maude, carefully picking through them as if it made a difference which order he took them. "Is there really peyote in those emeralds?" Hippie inquired.

"You see the smoke, right? You smell it, don't you," Maude answered as she sniffed the smoke.

"My nose is pretty stuffed, so I don't smell it, but yeah, I see the smoke, although it seems cleaner than normal smoke. Where is it lit?"

"The smoke is a fragrance. It don't need to be lit." She took in another whiff.

Hippie sniffed, too, but not with much gusto. He was uncertain what the peyote would do to him, especially if it counteracted the niacin oddly. Was peyote bad for your health or could it be medicinal? Did it enlighten your mind or kill brain cells? Did it have a lingering effect? He honestly didn't know any of those answers.

Oh, what the hell! he thought and took a stronger whiff to take in its odor. Except it had none. He would have been able to smell it by now. He gave Maude an inquisitive stare.

"Oh, yes, that's right. Peyote has no tangible smell. It's the smoke we're smellin'," she said, kind of admitting that her previous statement had been wrong. "That's what makes the peyote so good," she added offhand. "But even better is the cash I make from these emeralds." Maude snapped her fingers to let the ranger kid know that she wanted to hold one piece of her precious cargo.

The boy obliged by handing her the one he happened to have in his hand before going back to work. "Oh, what a beauty!" Now Maude seemed to be sniffing money instead of the odorless peyote.

"Will the peyote affect us since we are enclosed in such a small place without any windows?" Hippie asked, although he guessed at the answer by the way he was starting to feel.

"You bet!" Maude confirmed. "Just wait till the mescaline takes effect. Sometimes, I really do see money emitting from those emeralds."

"I'll soon be traveling back to the sixties or when the Native Americans ruled this land. A New-Age Hippie going back in time!"

"Peyote might induce hallucinations and has medicinal value, too. Stand away, weed!" Hippie wasn't sure if Maude was truly seeing the marijuana plants in a hallucination rather than the emerald, but she certainly had a glazed look in her eyes.

He felt a little something but was not yet seeing anything out of the ordinary. Perhaps the niacin was fighting the effects of the peyote.

Ranger boy had just about completed his work of gathering and bagging the peyote emeralds. He reached for the one on the table. "No—leave that one!" Maude screamed, turning toward him like a cheetah first spotting a gazelle. "That one's sacred."

Hippie observed the emerald on the table. At first, he had thought that all the emeralds were emanating a similar light, but now that this one stood alone, he could tell that it was the most powerful, for its light still bounced off the walls even without the others being there, and green smoke leapt off it like frogs jumping in ponds. The frogs were energized, too. They jumped and bounced and skipped all over the cabin, which expanded into beautiful green ponds with green waterlilies, avocado rocks, and olive dragonflies buzzing amongst the frogs. He thought he saw the dragonflies spread their winged dollar bill, flapping and whisking away the money.

Hippie glazed at the bag that Maude held. On the front of the sack was a green dollar sign, like you'd see in a bad cop and robber's vaudeville show—Maude was getting away with the loot!

The boy ranger, meanwhile, was gathering more loot from the treasure chest clubhouse. These were not peyote emeralds but other types of smaller rocks and wood and jewelry, which fit nicely in another green dollar signed sack. Maude grabbed this sack and then said to the ranger, "Great, and as agreed upon, you retain all rights to everything in the clubhouse, besides the remaining peyote emerald and anything made from petrified wood, on the condition they stay safe, of course. Happy spending!" With these words, they all departed the clubhouse of riches, and the albino lad padlocked the doors.

"I guess he's not staying at the clubhouse tonight," Maude said to Hippie. "He must be sleeping at the hammock house in the petrified woods."

Hippie was intrigued. He loved hammocks about as much as he loved niacin gardens. He had slept on quite a few hammocks in his time but never a whole hammock house. "What's that place like?" he had to ask.

But before she answered, Hippie heard a crunch of a branch, which alarmed Maude. "It's them!" she exclaimed.

"Who?"

"Them!" and she pointed to the brush. Carolyn and Bearman came out of their hiding place before Maude could catch them and beat them to a pulp. They were busted, and running from Maude could only lead to blood and mayhem. Bearman had seen it firsthand when his friends became human pretzels.

But it seemed that Jim had another reason not to run, "Jesus, please forgive our eavesdropping."

"Haven't we been over this?" Hippie replied, amused rather than annoyed.

"I am a reporter," Carolyn declared, convincing nobody. "What you have in there, Maude, must have been obtained illegally. That makes quite a story."

Maude laughed bitterly. "Nope to both your assessments. What I have was not stolen, and nope, you aren't no damned journo."

At that moment, Hippie did something he hadn't done in a very long time: he supported Maude by confronting someone who had not challenged him first. "Carolyn, you've never shown any evidence of being a reporter. Do you have any identification supporting your claim?" he asked, weakly challenging her.

"I am a reporter. Better than any journo you ever met, Maude," Carolyn said with a bravado that Hippie did not find convincing, especially since she still had not provided something like an AP press pass to help make her case.

"I'm not familiar with reporting jargon, but I believe that you first learned the word 'journo' when Maude said it." Hippie didn't much care about reporting lingo, but he suspected that Carolyn didn't either. "And you still haven't given us any proof of your profession. Who are you, really?" he asked, now giving her the puppy dog furrow of his eyebrows. Few women could resist telling him the truth when he did that. He didn't do it often, though, because he rarely cared whether the truth was being spoken or not. What difference did it make to him? He would live his life carefree no matter what lies might be told. He suspected, however, that he had mostly been told the truth throughout his life for precisely that reason. People tended to open-up to him because he had a friendly face, and he always listened. The Jesus appearance helped, too.

"And who are you, really?" he repeated.

"Carolyn," Carolyn said, because it was her real name after all, although that was not precisely what Hippie had been asking her.

"Jim." Bearman stated a second after Carolyn.

"Yes, go on," Hippie said, sympathetically.

"Jim," Bearman repeated. Then added, "You are my savior, Jesus." He looked as if he were about to bow to him again, but Hippie stayed his hand, telling him to stop his reverence.

Well, at least Jim had not been pretending.

Meanwhile, Carolyn softened as Hippie gave her that look that said, "Please tell the truth."

"I'm no reporter," Carolyn admitted, finally unable to carry forth the lie any longer while also acquiescing to Hippie's charming expression. "I'm an out-of-work actress and hairdresser." Hippie could see the relief in her face as the truth came out at last.

"But would you rather hear that I need blood to quench my thirst?" Was she joking, or was this some insane ploy to detract from her lie?

"Why are you here, Carolyn?" Hippie asked, ignoring her last question, because it was just an insane attempt to change the subject, and he instinctively knew that the truth would come out now.

And Carolyn burst out yelling, "I love George Cramwell!"

Chapter 20
Bloodshedder's Soulmate

George Cramwell heard Jade holler his name, but he could not respond, not right now. He had some thinking to do and was still recovering from the hot air balloon ride from Hell. Not that the balloon journey had been the worst thing to make him ill recently. The breakup with Jade had been no picnic; the main reason for the separation made his stomach hurl.

He hadn't done anything wrong. Really, it was true. He hadn't cheated. That woman was just plain nuts, totally bonkers, out of her mind. He had barely known her. Maybe he had seen her once or twice, that was all, although she may have been stalking him. She sure had spoken crap to Jade, too. He had only brushed up against that woman once, in passing, hardly seeing her. There had been no other contact whatsoever, let alone sex.

I was faithful. I still would be faithful. I'm a good man. At least George told himself that.

However ridiculous this whole adventure had been thus far, at least it had gotten George far away from Carolyn. Jade said that the woman had moved to California. But how did she really know? From what a crazy person said. And even if Carolyn had moved, Wyoming certainly wasn't California. Perhaps he'd just move here. Alone. Get away from everything else. Perhaps it was his destiny to live in Wyoming. That's why he had somewhat willingly ventured on this journey, an unconscious path to his fate.

The balloon ride had played a part of his journey and he could have been fine with that, but after rising a hundred feet in the air, he had realized that he was deathly afraid of heights. He had never been in a plane or even atop a roof of a building, so he had not known, although his subconscious had never allowed him to face his fear. Hence, the fear took over so that he could barely move during the entire terrorizing trip, nearly frozen like a human icicle.

This whole trip, especially the voyage on the hot air balloon, was *"Ridicula"*. To George Cramwell, the invented word meant: *extremely ridiculous but somehow plausible*. For instance, most balloons traveled around thirty-five kilometers, such as the distance from New York City to New Rochelle. His trip had lasted more than double that, but that distance was certainly not out of the realm of possibility, especially with the involvement of inclement weather. He had experienced it, so he knew. And he had been through a lot since New York, and it had been largely ridicula.

But now he was down in Wyoming. He had seen the park map; he sort of knew his whereabouts.

In any case, he was away from that woman, for sure. Carolyn could not possibly trace him here.

Why Jade was convinced that this woman had been his mistress was still a bit of mystery to him, for their final conversation as a couple had not enlightened him much. It had gone something like this:

"How dare you cheat on me?" Jade had come roaring into his workplace like a train into a tunnel. Everyone in the little office stared, but she didn't care. Having a few hairs out of place on her head was embarrassing, but this was only his pathetic marketing job, so it meant nothing to her.

"Huh?"

"You're such an ass. You and that bitchy hairdresser being all lovey-dovey," Jade said. "And that Caroline, or whatever her name is, does not hold a candle to me."

"Huh?" he repeated. "What hairdresser?"

"I know you're good at it, but stop acting dumb and just accept that we're over." She stomped down her heel and then slapped him like lightning on the face.

He smarted but managed to say, "I don't know what you're talking about."

But the brief discussion about his supposed misconduct was over. She stormed out like booming thunder.

He had been too stunned to go after her. All he heard was the knucklehead salesman in the next cubicle say, "Dude, that was your girlfriend? Wow! And you had another hottie on the side? Righteous!"

Only later would he find out who the woman was that Jade had been convinced he had been cheating with. But the why was still hazy. He and Carolyn had only met a few times since that first time in passing. And still, he had never had any romantic inclinations toward her. He did not have interest in Carolyn, mainly because she was nuts. Bat-crazy!

He had tried to find out more about the situation by going to Carolyn's workplace. And yes, he had been stupid enough to let her cut his hair. Before she attempted the haircut, she began talking about vampires and sucking his blood. After she pricked him with the scissors on the neck, presumably to taste his blood, he had run from the salon like a bat out of hell, his protective hair gown still on, drips of blood oozing from neck to gown.

Bloodshedder! That's who she was, and that had become his nickname for Carolyn.

In the following few weeks, he had had no more encounters with Carolyn, thankfully. As for Jade, they rarely saw each other and never talked after their breakup. He couldn't find any words that would set things right because she would not believe him anyway. He was not even sure he had wanted reconciliation, for their relationship had not been going well. She was too materialistic, and he had no money to spend on her. She had her trust issues while he was carefree. He liked the simple things while she was more intellectual. For instance, she liked foreign, not action movies. Enough said!

Yet, they had gotten together because she had found him funny and endearing, and he had found her to be sophisticated and attractive. They had laughed it up at Kenny's party, where they had met. Why couldn't they laugh now? Everything since that awkward breakup had been surreal, and these past few days had been outright ridicula. Yet here they were near but still so far apart.

First out of the balloon—because he had been thrown like a skydiver without a parachute into the bushes—he had just lain there not ready to get up and wanting to stay hidden. He needed to compose himself, and he couldn't help feeling a tad bit responsible for the mess they were in.

Thankfully, neither Jade nor the others had found him yet. That left him more time for his heart to stop racing.

But someone else had. He knew this because he heard a woman yelling his first and last names. At first, he thought it was Jade, but he quickly realized that it could not be her for three reasons: 1) It hadn't sounded like Jade; 2) The shriek came from the opposite direction than where Jade would be; and most notably, 3) This woman shouted that she loved him. Jade would shout commands, obscenities, and jokes at him but never that word.

George laughed. He had to be hearing things. The sound must have been that of an eagle overhead, and he had only imagined it to be a woman's voice. Come on, who would shout that she loved HIM?

Then he heard even louder, "That's right. I LOVE George Hemmingway Cramwell!" Who the hell knew his middle name? He was no drunken famous author, so he found no reason to ever use his middle name, not even the H.

"Who's there?" Jade yelled. She had heard the other woman's voice this time, so he couldn't have imagined it, even if he were Hemmingway drunk.

"You show yourself first," said a different, rougher woman's voice. "You better be just passing by."

Jade began to say something but then shut her mouth. She wasn't about to face off with strangers. She was not much for continued confrontation, just initial mocking, and she certainly wouldn't show herself without shoes and perfectly combed hair, unless she just wanted to tell off George.

That ship sailed when a bulky woman came crashing through the brush, just narrowly missing bulldozing George in his hiding place. "You've been following us too, woman?" she said, suddenly up close and personal with Jade.

Jade cowered, and the men froze, watching. They would be too late to help Jade if the large, bulky woman threw a fist, and George was manly enough to admit that he was scared of the broad woman, too. *That woman's a brute!*

Courageous little Maria, however, stepped forward, branch waving in hand, ready to strike. "Step back!" she strongly commanded. "No need for fighting. We had no idea you were around."

Surprisingly, the gigantic woman (she looked bigger every time George blinked) did back up. "Sorry. I get headstrong when around my stuff."

At that moment, three men fell into George's view. The first looked more hair than man. The second looked more boy than man and had no hair. The third had hair like Jesus....

It couldn't be! No way! Then George recalled that it could really be him since George currently precided in Wyoming.

It must be Hippie! Ridicula!

George began to move out of hiding when he received a soft tap on the shoulder. It seemed that Jade had finally found him, so he thought of a quick excuse that would explain why he had been hiding. He whirled around and said, "I was taking a dump!"

"You still smell good even with your crap somewhere near," Carolyn said. "Now let's see if you taste as good." She bent over, her mouth open, aiming to bite his neck.

"Bloodshedder! Get away!" George screamed so loud that Faulkner might have heard him in Jersey. He pushed his hands out, swinging them in a slap motion, like a girl on the playground, keeping her mouth at bay until he could stand up and run.

"From the first minute I saw you walking with that chick over there, I knew I had to make you mine. We could roam the nights together, enjoying each other's blood, fucking at leisure, never tiring, always free. You see, you are my mate. I felt it instantly as soon as I saw you." Carolyn had a ravished look on her face, lovelorn, as if he were the only one who could satisfy her.

"What the hell are you talking about? Is this what you told Jade?" he said, ready to bolt when he realized that his hands were no longer deterring her.

"Oh, that phony woman over there," she replied, pointing at Jade as a toddler might to a toy. "No, she wouldn't understand all that. I just told her the truth: that you and I are in love and that there was nothing she could do about it."

"You're fucking crazy!" and he bolted from her grasp. George did not look back. His only aim was to escape. Unfortunately, he wasn't looking ahead either. He smashed hard into a tree and keeled over.

Carolyn laughed demonically. "I'm coming to get you, my love. I need to suck your sweet blood so that we can live forever in seductive ecstasy! I am your succubus!"

George could not stand back up. Whether stunned or injured, he wasn't certain. He tried to roll to freedom, but the ground had a slight incline, so he wound up rolling back toward Carolyn.

"Rollerboy, no need to hurry to me. I'll be right there to pleasure you!" And she was right on top of him seconds later.

"Your blood, honey! Your blood, Sweetie! Your blood, Soulmate!" George saw her red fiery eyes and lush sinful lips—a vampire in heat! When she bit, would he turn into Bloodshedder's permanent soulmate?

Holy hell! But he was resigned to his fate.

Chapter 21
The Grand Fetcher Escapade: The End of the Ultimate Chase

MOOC scratched every corner of the crate he found himself in without it budging. It was secure. He could not escape that way.

But he could escape by going under it. Martens were not known for their digging and tunneling ability, but Rascally Rascal was no ordinary pine marten. He prided himself on burrowing better than a rabbit or gopher and tunneling quicker than a Russell Terrier.

That dog and his oddball crew had shown some cleverness, but MOOC would outmaneuver them. He clawed the soil, found it soft, and began digging at top speed. He'd be gone before that Rottweiler could bring his clumsy body over to appraise his catch, especially since he had already built an intricate maze of tunnels underneath the Douglas-fir. After all, the tree was one of his favorite hideouts.

All he had to do was dig to the point where he could intercept one of the tunnels. This turned out to be easier than he had thought; a tunnel presented itself before he had dug a meter deep.

That dog was in for a surprise. When it opened his trap, it would find that remarkable Rascally Rascal had escaped.

That dog, Freckles, lumbered underneath Grand Fetcher at that very moment and spotted the box. He had been careful not to become entangled in the tree, and since he was a rather large dog, this had taken some considerable effort.

But it would be all worth it. His nemesis was caught, thanks to the hummingbirds that had flown through the area at precisely the right moment before moving on. The cat and the man had done their jobs, too, albeit clumsily, which was expected from them anyway.

Now it was time to mock that marten incessantly. He thought about a cartoon that Harrison liked, involving a coyote and roadrunner. What would Wile E. Coyote say to the roadrunner if he ever caught it? The dog was not sure, but he was ready to say his zinger anyway.

"Cawabunga!" he barked as he looked in the crate.

He did not see any marten. Dammit! Had he not caught that marten after all? Then he saw the hole in the ground. That marten had dug himself free. And set a record pace at that.

What a mischievous, cunning, and resourceful rascal that marten was!

But Freckles still had a few tricks of his own and was not a dog who gave up. In that way and maybe only in that way, he was like a Chihuahua. Their unwillingness to give up was the reason they yapped so much. *Annoying but respectable.*

Now where would the marten go? He knew that rascal would not be far off. It would rather tease him than escape. It was just a matter of where and when he showed up rather than if. Therefore, Freckles decided to wait rather than run around aimlessly searching, which could be a fun activity but not worth his energy at the moment.

"What's wrong with you, you mutt?" Harrison yelled crankily. Was it naptime for the old man already? That was usually the time the man called Freckles "mutt," because normally he knew that the dog that lived in his home was a full-bred Rottweiler—and proud of it.

"Aren't you going after that smart-aleck marten in the box?" the man continued. How little did that man observe. The marten would likely be back to scare him. *Ridicula!* But Freckles would never be scared by a little pine marten.

"Where did that darn cat go?" Harrison asked. Well, at least he had observed that. *That cat was probably meowing her way home. Scaredy cat!*

Before Freckles heard any more complaints from his so-called owner, the marten came from out of the ground right below Harrison's feet, which caused him to drop the weed whacker as he yelped in surprise. The whacker had whacked its last weed, for it broke in half on a rock.

Freckles saw the smirk. That marten was laughing it up. The old man may be a clumsy bumbler, but he did not deserve that treatment. Freckles charged after that smartass marten.

The race and chase was on again. *Bring it on, marten!*

They skirted through brush and bramble, tree and branch, rock and crevice. They never tired, and the marten egged the dog on. Harrison, on the other hand, gave chase for only a few steps and then already winded, said, "Fuck this damn chase. Don't like 'em in action movies so not gonna do it now," he muttered, but Freckles heard him with his uncanny hearing. "I'm going home. Maybe get me some lox and herring and perhaps take an early nap—" The man muttered some more, but Freckles became intent on the chase and left Harrison to his own blundering ways.

The marten ran up a hill. As he reached higher ground he climbed toward the edge, where the area was unstable for Freckle's four feet and large frame. The dog did not immediately see a hanging ledge and nearly tumbled over it. One paw already dropping, he recovered his hind legs enough to keep traction and remain climbing. That marten was trying to make him fall and had almost succeeded. *That devilish scoundrel!*

When they reached the summit and ran down on the other side, Freckles gained on the smaller marten. As the terrain levelled, he nearly had his nemesis, inches from him. The Rottweiler nipped at the marten's tail, teeth expecting to nab the marten, but instead he bit air. And his teeth grinding hurt!

The marten had whipped his tail away and then zagged to the right, narrowly missing an old stump of a tree. Freckles could not stop in time but could jump the stump. He did so, but the marten had gained a lead once more.

In midair, Freckles realized just how much fun he was having. And the marten had given this delight to him. That marten might be a fiendish pain in the butt and had tried to injure and mock him over and over again, but he sure was good for some good ole entertainment.

The race and chase persisted. They must have covered many kilometers, so Freckles no longer knew where in Yellowstone he traveled. The terrain was completely unfamiliar to him. Perhaps it was time to give up and find his way home before he became too lost to even guess where to go. He began to slow.

The marten looked back at him and gave him a wry smile. This did what it had intended; it incited the Rottweiler. Freckles' pace quickened. He would catch this rascal even if he needed to run to

Colorado. At one point, he didn't notice when he instinctively skirted by a woman, not seeing her lose her balance.

The sun was up in the sky, dawn left behind, when he saw his next chance to grab hold of the marten's tail, but this time he did not nip haphazardly. He watched the tail's movement instead, focusing, trying to strike and not miss. He recognized the motion; he had it timed. His nemesis was caught!

Except just as he struck, a different woman somehow appeared out of nowhere between the marten and Freckles. He had been so intent on catching the marten he had not seen her at all. He had no choice but to slam into her, and the result would not be pretty.

Boom! She screamed and fell hard one way while Freckles flew the other. He landed in a heap right next to a man sprawled out on the ground.

Needless to say, the marten escaped, and Freckles could imagine him chuckling with his mocking grin in doing so. Yet, the dog was not upset or angry about it.

Because that chase had been so much fun, and the dog knew that the marten would be waiting for more fun.

Chapter 22
Seventies or Eighties Music

Hippie looked at the lunacy around him. He saw new faces and animals and nature but could not be certain whether any of it was reality or just a cartoon in his imagination. The peyote, possibly made more potent because of the niacin in his system, made him see things. What he saw was all with nature, of course, but he never realized that the branches of oaks and maple trees could be so long. They seemed to be reaching out to him, inviting him to join them in harmonious tree singing, but he knew better. He had seen the movies and read the books: they wanted to capture and squeeze his bones dry. And those dogwoods wished to cover him with pretty white flowers to suffocate him. And those Redwoods—forget about it!

"Dogwood, dogwood," he began to sing, remembering an old childhood song that had always calmed him, and as he sang, his paranoia faded. The dogwood trees were beautiful once more, their leaves no longer threatening. However, his hallucinations resumed; he tripped hard!

First, he thought he saw his old buddy, George Cramwell, appear out of thin air only to trip in front of one of the aforementioned dogwood trees. Then he witnessed Carolyn change into a bloodthirsty, lovelorn succubus whose only wish was to abduct George and make him her plaything. Before she could reach him, though, a dog chasing some smaller critter came barreling through, causing Carolyn to lose her balance. As she fell, time seemed to stand still for a moment. Hippie saw every inch of her body collapse, split apart, and then reform into a woman's figure once more, suddenly looking like an angel rather than a succubus, woman rather than spawn, normal rather than crazy. Hippie knew he must still be tripping, for Carolyn was certainly not normal by any means. He had known that fact from when they first met all those days ago. Still, he liked her no matter what lunacy she stirred up. That's why he liked Maude and Bearman and

George, too, although he still could not be certain this was George and not a hallucination that lay before him.

Slapping George lightly on the cheek brought him to his senses. "Oww!" he said.

Hippie guessed that the slap had been harder than he had thought, for the red mark persisted many seconds afterward. Of course, this was against his nonviolent nature. He wasn't Maude, after all.

Before he apologized, though, George (he was reasonably sure that it was indeed him) said. "Is that you? The great man himself and my friend?"

At first Hippie thought that he had knocked George into Bearman's way of thinking or that the real Jesus was standing behind him. Then he realized that George's adoring look was strictly for him, Hippie. George had always worshipped him just a little bit, although his friend knew him not to be anything like Jesus. Hippie did have that effect on people, although he could not fathom why.

But George's expression quickly changed. "Look out!"

A small weasel (for Hippie was one of the few that knew that martens were not rodents) raced by his feet. He skipped out of its way just to almost be pummeled over by the return of the Rottweiler. At that moment, Hippie had to be a little more athletic, so he became Sportsman Aspen. Diving out of the way, skidding on the flowers of the dogwood and jumping back to his feet unhurt and unblemished, took all of Aspen's dexterity. The funny thing was that for an instant he still saw his Hippie self, attempting to reason with the dog instead of leaping out of the way. Had the peyote truly made him two people: Hippie and Aspen finally escaping the one body? Was he now in his spiritual body? But then his view of his other self-dissolved from his perception, and he was one person again, although even in his current state, he was pretty sure his two selves had never really separated. He would have to test his perspective with some meditation, but right now he had to figure out what the hell was going on.

Because he saw flying zombies approaching!

First, Hippie (for now his Aspen spirit had returned to his Hippie body) saw a mustache on an Italian body moving dizzily toward him, like a tired zombie walking nearly sideways rather than forward, and the mustache seemed to be leading the way. His hair was disheveled, his face looked thin and gaunt, and he reeked. Hippie could smell him from where he stood. Yet, his mustache was immaculate.

Behind him bowed a half man, for he was facing the ground as he walked, looking as if he would belch at any moment. He was either hungover, still drunk, extremely seasick on land, drugged out, or a zombie. Then Hippie noticed the wreck of a deflated hot air balloon nearby, which made him realize that none of the above was true. This man was airsick on land.

In his condition and because he had seen these two men first, Hippie understood why he had truly thought them zombies, but the two women he now saw certainly looked human. Except that one of them had just survived a hot air balloon crash but still looked flawless. Not one tress of hair was out of place, and while she may not have been wearing makeup, she might as well have been. The only evidence that she had been in an accident was that her feet were scratched up because she wore no shoes. Hippie noticed that immediately. Shoes and feet could tell a lot about a person, but in this case, this lady was so out of her element that her banged up feet told him nothing.

The Latin lady looked more comfortable, perhaps because she wore shoes, or rather, upscale New Yorker sneakers. Immediately, Hippie could tell that she was the cool one of the group. She held this ragtag team together, for none of these others could be leaders. They could barely be assistants to this suave woman. And if George came with this group, he would fit in with the followers. George was a great guy, but he was no leader.

"Come here, doggie," the female leader was saying, but the Rottweiler was not listening, determined to find the marten that had slipped from his view again, but Hippie saw the critter taunting the dog from behind him.

Hippie stared at the marten, recognizing that rascally rascal. He had seen him a few times in his many trips to Wyoming and Yellowstone. That marten was nicknamed MOOC, and he was awesome! Plus, if he were picking on the dog, the Rottweiler must be a fantastic competitor to MOOC's fun mischievousness.

But because of his competitive clumsiness, the dog made a huge mistake: he tried to take a shortcut when turning around and running towards MOOC, thereby nearly colliding with Maude. Anybody else in the vicinity would have attempted to avoid the big dog, but Maude was a different story. She stood her ground, and the dog slammed into her like an oncoming train heading into a station on the wrong track. However, the Rottweiler did not collapse or even whimper. Instead, he just bounced off the falling woman and veered to the left, knocking a bag from her hand in the process before moving on.

And so, the peyote emeralds tumbled to the ground, creating a frenzy of hallucinogenic greed, sort of like how the United States operated today. The immaculate woman succumbed quickly to the temptation, likely out of curiosity and her love of shiny new things rather than the effects of the peyote acting as perfume or out of sheer greed. But that curiosity was the American way when it came to jewelry or money. And the emeralds were green.

"Stop, Jade!" the Latin woman said. "What are you doing?" Hippie could see right away that practical cautiousness overruled presumptuousness with this lady.

"Helping this woman retrieve her stuff." But neither her friend, Hippie, or Maude were fooled. Jade just wanted to see the shiny stuff. After all, she was named after a shiny stone, so the love of gaudy emeralds must be in her family's genes.

Ranger boy interceded before Maude recovered enough to be ready to deal with this meddling woman. "That's Maude's property," he said weakly, as he might if he were defending a kid against a bully. But Maude certainly didn't need any protection.

Jade ignored the albino-like boy and reached to pick up an emerald.

"I'm not sure if that's wise," Hippie said. He would have normally kept quiet, but the peyote was making him garrulous.

"Better listen to Jesus!" Bearman boomed from across the glade. He stood from a kneeling position, positioned two fingers like a cross, and tapped them to his heart. While the Hippie part of him would not know, his Aspen portion related Jim's motion to that of Tim Tebow in his football years. (Who knows? Perhaps Time Tebow did this before he played baseball games, too.)

Had Jim been interrupted from a prayer? Had he been praying to Hippie?

Maude, whose unpredictability of whether she'd fight or cope was unparalleled, decided to do a little of both this time. She reared back to take a swing at Jade but stopped within centimeters of her nose. "Made you flinch," she said, sounding like a jovial juvenile.

The fact that Jade hadn't flinched didn't escape Hippie's notice, and he dared not bring that to Maude's attention even in his current state. But not flinching was only the first unprecedented thing that Jade did, because then she ignored Maude and walked off with the emerald, as if Maude weren't there. *That woman had balls!*

"Come back here!" cried Maude, sounding like a wounded animal rather than a fearsome predator.

"I've been walking mostly on my bare feet for days," Jade responded. "This ornament can help pay for that misery. Thank you very much."

Maude looked incredulous. How could this immaculate woman with no shoes talk to her like that? But Maude didn't pound her for her insolence. Instead, she laughed. "Must be the peyote. It affects each person in different ways."

When Jade kept walking, Maude continued, "Oh, what the hell? Take it. I have plenty more."

And just like that, any potential feud was forgotten. Maybe they'd all get along. Hippie liked the thought. After all, peace was what he was all about. He would have played his guitar in celebration, if he still owned one and had a thimble. But nevertheless, he still heard music—birds were chirping, and the wind played Bob Dylan's "Blowin' in the Wind," at least in his peyote-soaked head.

The song of the wind in his mind changed to "Sledgehammer" by Peter Gabriel when he heard the bang, then to "Silent Running" by Mike and the Mechanics when he perceived but not quite heard someone running behind him, and then finally to "St. Elmo's Fire" when he smelt smoke in the air. St. Elmo's Fire rang in his head with such clarity that he actually remembered who sang it: John Parr. What was happening? What eighties Hell was this? Hippie had thought his mind would stick to all the great seventies music no matter what. With peyote, however, the eighties invaded.

Instead of worrying about music, Hippie should have been more aware of what was happening around him. That's because the sledgehammer bang was Freckles smashing into Maude's clubhouse while MOOC escaped underneath. Subsequently, greenish smoke seeped from the clubhouse, which caused Maude and the boy ranger to run toward their precious house of treasures while everyone else retreated.

But all this commotion that all of this made was not silent. The running that Hippie had perceived did not have anything to do with the clubhouse, for now he saw that Carolyn had recovered and was running toward her prized possession: George.

Hippie was torn. Where should he go? What could he do? In any case he had to revert from peaceful Hippie to Sportsman or even up to Superhero Aspen (the highest Aspen level), although they were all one and the same, but he felt more confident when splitting himself up in these terms. He didn't have a split personality. He just was a creative, spirited soul.

Just as Carolyn reached poor hapless George, Aspen grabbed her arms and flipped her onto his back. Then he tried to fly away with her still intact, for the peyote made him think that this was possible. Of course, the flying ended up being a jump, and Carolyn's weight made him tumble upon his landing. He lost his grip of her, preferring to protect himself from injury rather than continuing to hold her. Suffice to say, Carolyn escaped and resumed her quest to torment George.

"Are you all right?" the Latina woman asked as he sat back up after his fall.

Never embarrassed, he responded, "That was just the beginning—"

But the man who had looked drunk when Hippie had first seen him interrupted his repartee. "Maria, come quick!" the man, now definitely sounding sober, said from close by.

Now what?

"How dare you take my emerald?" Jade was saying to the mustached man. Somehow, the emerald was now officially hers. "You can never have it. She's my baby!" But stranger than what she said was the fact that the man wasn't even holding the emerald. She still had it cupped in her left hand.

"What's wrong here?" Maria asked when she arrived on the scene. Hippie crept up more cautiously because Jade looked like she could strike anyone at any time at any moment. "Bobarino, did you try to steal the emerald?"

The mustached Italian shrugged, admitting no guilt. "Is there something in that thing?" he asked, pointing to the emerald. "She's acting crazy even for her."

"She's one of those," Maude interjected as she came from somewhere Hippie had not noticed, grabbed Jade, loosened her grip of the emerald without much effort even though Jade had been holding onto it for dear life, and tossed it in Hippie's direction. "Paranoia is a rare side effect of this particular strain of peyote," Maude explained as Hippie caught the prize.

"Give it back. Give back my emerald. And I want my shoe!" Jade said.

"Guess she's got the hallucinations too," Maude added.

Although Hippie now held the emerald and Maude had been the one to confiscate it, Jade attacked Bobarino, punching at him like an angered lover unwilling to actually hurt her beloved. Her Italian man just took the soft blows. He seemed not to know what else to do.

Of all things, a fly subverted Jade's wrath. She must have seen it from the corner of her eye, for she started to wave around, attempting to swat additional imaginary flies, because there was only one buzzing around. She began to run in fear. "Fly away you flies! Get away from me! Especially that one with the orange nose!" She ran twenty paces, turned around to see that the fly (flies) had gone, and calmed.

Meanwhile, the emerald began to radiate and then pulsate in Hippie's hands like a green alien's heart. Then light protruded from it like a green X-ray. Was he hallucinating this effect? At this point, he could barely tell reality from his imagination, but he was kind of leaning towards this being real.

Subsequently, the pulsating began to pound his hand like a mallet beating under his skin, and the imaginary mallet seemed to pinch a nerve in his hand, because suddenly the pulsation crept up the nerves in his arms until it reached his shoulder. From there, it reverberated through the rest of his body—through artery, vein, capillary, and whatever else his blood coursed through. Thus, he felt the rhythm in his entire body, including his brain, where the true creative outlet lingered. From there, his pulsating inspiration traveled out through his ears in musical and effervescent bliss.

If anyone or everyone (except perhaps the dog and marten) saw the emerald light beam toward the clubhouse, Hippie could not be certain, but he did see, feel, hear, and smell (although odorless) the peyote ray permeating through the cracks of the wood. He became one with the emerald, somehow a temporary bond stronger than that he had with the niacin. He felt whole, enlightened, purified. Thus, he let all the craziness around him dissolve as he found Zenlike meditation among chaos, eyes nearly shut so that he did not see, for he could only be.

Inside the clubhouse, the smoke briefly engulfed the light of the emerald which Hippie held to that of the lead emerald still lying on the table. He breathed in the smoke with gusto, generating a fruitfulness within him. For that moment, Hippie truly felt rich beyond merely seeing the monetary value of the emeralds, beyond the peace and relaxation that the meditation afforded him, beyond even the joy of life. That's because he knew that his calling was here, that he was about to embark on a mission to fulfill all human dreams and ambitions.

The smoke dissipated then, as the fiery emeralds lost their luster. And less than a second afterward, his mission ended as he saw only the blackness of one who had just passed out.

Chapter 23
Bloodshot Love

Carolyn took only an instant to recover from the attack of the crazy male angel who called himself Hippie or occasionally Aspen. She knew he could cause some hassle but was no real threat. He could keep her away from her purpose temporarily, but she would always track her target. That Neanderthal Maude woman couldn't stop her, either. After all, they couldn't derail destiny, for the train would keep rolling even when off track. She had taken a delayed train but had finally reached her destination. George would be carried off in her caboose.

She reached the fallen one, ready to make him hers. He had just come to, for he moved his arms to welcome her embrace. His hands were held out, seemingly to keep her at bay, but she knew he would widen them when he realized that their destiny was at hand. She would be his wife and his demoness lover. What more could he ask for?

"Bloodshedder!" he yelled when he was alert enough to see her. He was complimenting her, for the one who sheds blood with the most passion and love shall be the mistress of all mistresses, the wife of all wives, and the seductress of all seductresses all in one. She was his Lilith, and he was her Adam.

"Stay away," he said and put his hands together like a cross.

She laughed seductively and then said, "Please, Husband. Let us bind with blood!" She clawed at his neck then. One of her long nails scraped her own neck, drawing a smidgeon of blood. That same nail avoided his hands and punctured his neck, releasing his delicious blood. Thus, they bled together and were blood-linked.

"Was that so hard?" she asked as she drew him in to suck more blood from his neck.

When Carolyn first clawed his neck, George felt a quick stinging pain, as if from a wasp or a spider's bite. The resulting dripping of blood felt like muddy water dripping down a ravine and plopping into a puddle below. He instantly trembled, ready to faint, but the queasiness passed as his and Carolyn's blood condensed together on his neck, somehow putting him at ease, so much so as a matter of fact, that the blending of blood began to feel like a balm of soothing warmth and comfort, as if a part of him forever.

Fear left him as she drew him in for a second serving of his blood, which somehow soothed him more. He still faced a crazy woman, for she was Bloodshedder, but he didn't mind that title so much now. Weren't we all a bit crazy? After all he had been through, he had to be daft anyway to find himself in this situation.

So, she thought she was a vampire? Maybe I could be her incubus? Wouldn't that be ridicula?

Then his thoughts changed as doubt returned. Was that her blood upon his neck speaking for him? Was he that hard up for passion that he would allow a stalking loon to possess his will?

But she was pretty in her own bloodsucking, ferocious way. And she obviously liked him!

When she spoke again, asking, "Was that so hard?" George barely heard her, but he responded with an inappropriate signal—he got hard!

"I guess so," Carolyn was close enough to feel his physical change. "My blood got to your pecker already. Now you will react to me forever!"

He guessed that he would.

She took one last taste of his blood, pulled him against her clothing, and ripped his tattered T-shirt. Licking her lips hungrily, she began tearing at her own blouse.

Then someone tackled her.

If George had been expecting someone to tackle his stalking lover, he would have thought it to be anyone other than the normally timid Kenny. Hippie would try to break up what he deemed to be a fight. Maria had peaceful aura but a fiery demeanor. George would have hoped that Jade still had a bit of jealous rage in her. The rest, even the boy ranger, surely had more initiative than Kenny. But here he was wrestling Carolyn off him, which quickly deterred his torrid horniness.

"You bitch devil, get off my friend!" Kenny yelled, not seeing or understanding what had really been happening.

Carolyn rolled away from him before turning back, lifting her fingers and thrusting her nails at him like Catwoman on the prowl. Her eyes had seemingly changed from lustful bloodshot red to vengeful shadowy black. Her lips purred incomprehensible words that were laced with menace. Her ears perked out like a stereotypical elf. Her hair spiked up, electrified by some cosmic energy. In other words, she looked angry as hell.

Surprisingly Kenny did not back off, or the threat had not yet penetrated his addled brain. What had happened to him? Had he found more alcohol to drink? Then George saw a peyote emerald in his hand. That explained it. He was probably seeing Carolyn as a she-kitten rather than an angered madwoman. "Bring it on, little lady!" Kenny exclaimed.

"No, Kenny" George intervened, his hands trying to block the two off each other. "It's not necessary."

Neither Kenny nor George's crazily lovable new girlfriend listened to him. Instead, they each were sizing each other up, looking to pounce.

"Don't hurt him," George continued to Carolyn even though he knew her to be too angry to listen, but he also realized that his friend was no match for his next girlfriend, Carolyn, drugged or not.

Carolyn didn't listen to him, as expected. Instead, she clawed at Kenny and would have skewered his face if it weren't for George's intervention. He lifted his head intentionally to take the brunt of the piercing from Carolyn's nails. He immediately began to rain blood from both of his cheeks.

Bloodshedder had struck again.

"Oh, my poor kine mortal, my future fledgling, my love. You bleed when I didn't intend it." Remorse replaced anger; George had unwittingly deflated her fury. Meanwhile, Kenny had found enough sense in his drug-induced mind to retreat from harm's way.

Thankfully, George's gouges were not too serious. Thus, the blood mostly dried on his face rather than continued to drip down his neck. Carolyn took that relief as an invitation. She kissed him tenderly on the lips first, making George feel like she might mend his wounds with love. But that didn't last long, because then she licked the blood on his cheek and nipped at his neck, producing more blood. However, the pain only lasted a second, replaced by a tingling sensation, which aroused him.

Carolyn watched his arousal take place and smiled. "That kind of bite always works with blood soulmates. We shall now have to make savage love."

In response, George set it off—his keyring, that is. Flickers of color and the muzak of "Greased Lightning" briefly joined the party. *Appropriate. Sparks were flying!*

George would have been ready to give in to both of their desire, except for one major issue: not only was Kenny still watching them, but so was the rest of the ragtag team of humans.

Kenny was dumbfounded, or just plain dumb-looking.

Maria watched in disbelief, and the hairy man knelt next to her in some odd ritualistic prayer.

Bobarino turned off his keyring, laughed, and high-fived a frowning Maude, as if his soccer team had finally scored a goal.

Jade looked angry or jealous or neither. George couldn't tell. That's how much he had really known her.

But George did not see Hippie anywhere.

Chapter 24
Doggy Joy

Freckles realized that it was still morning, but he had been running and crashing and tromping to dizzying effect in his chase of the marten. So, he was tired—even exhausted.

He realized that even with all his tricks and guile, which took much effort, MOOC wasn't any better off. It was well past the pine marten's bedtime. After all, pine martens were mostly nocturnal animals. Freckles knew that much from his recent observations of the creature.

Thus, it was time for a truce, at least until the next and likely not last game of Chase commenced. But how was he going to tell the marten of this temporary truce? All the marten had communicated to him thus far was as an adversary, often in the form of mockery.

Yet a strange kind of bonding between equal competitors had taken place during the chases. Normally he wouldn't ever want a truce when the business had not been finished, but a perfect adversary, even nemesis, had turned into good fun and promised further escapades in the future. He doubted the marten would say that it had found its Chase competitor as its equal, but a temporary truce was an admittance of a sort.

The chase had yet again raced its way back to the Grand Fetcher. It seemed that the Douglass-fir tree was the place where a truce would be had or not, and he had come up with an idea. Freckles stopped short of the tree, thus ending abruptly his current pursuit of the rascally rascal.

From under the tree the marten peaked its head out with a droll look, as if asking, "What is it, Fool?"

The dog lifted its paw in response, signaling a pause in action. Then Freckles lay down, though his eyes remained alert, staring directly at the marten.

The marten chuckled in its adversarial way, but then he also lay down. The critter had had enough this morning, too.

Thus, a truce had been struck.

***

MOOC had to give that brute of a dog some credit. He had matched him every step of the chase. That didn't mean that the marten couldn't get the best of him if he really wanted, but sometimes a good adversary in his games was better than embarrassing the dog so much that he wouldn't compete again. Plus, he had to admit that it was time to stop, because it was well past his bedtime.

However, he had one more little trick to play before he retired for the day. And it had nothing to do with the big dog. During the chase, he had run across a friend who he had to waylay in a playful manner. After all, Hippie deserved a shout out.

MOOC left his great Douglas-fir Christmas tree behind to search out his friend. He had not been surprised to see him because the man always found his way back to Wyoming, and he was past due in these parts of the state. What was surprising was that he was not visiting alone this time. MOOC could not ascertain about why he had those nincompoop companions with him.

After traversing the immediate area for some time, the marten found his quarry, but not in the way he expected. Blinded by a ray of light for an instant, he bumped right into his friend. The good thing was that he was alone, but the bad thing was that he lay asleep, possibly comatose.

That also meant that his plan to scare him would not work. MOOC was mostly sure that men had to be awake to be startled.

Rascally Rascal could not help trying, however. He scampered to his face only inches away and gave the man his best scary face he could muster with his eyes wide and his claws up.

Nothing.

But then something happened that he had not expected because he had not realized that the brute dog was still in the vicinity. Not looking or uncaring, the dog blasted into Hippie, like a bull into a blaze of red. This woke Hippie with a start.

The first thing that the man saw was MOOC directly in front of him. Hippie jumped up, freaked, scared to a pale white.

MOOC chuckled. He had gotten his wish after all, thanks to his partner in crime, his friend the Rottweiler, whose name he had no reason to ever find out.

Freckles knew that his rough-housing would do the trick, and he never meant the man any harm. He was rewarded when after his initial fright, the man, who he would soon find out to be the prodigious Hippie, began to laugh and playfully rough-house back. This man was awesome!
The pine marten also joined in his whimsical way, dancing around them like a pup first learning the intricacies of playful rough-housing. Yes, they were three very different animals having the best of fun.
And Freckles realized something more. This man was very similar to the dog: they both had a joyous quality that could never be contained.

Chapter 25
Contemplation

Upon the dog awakening him, Hippie seemed to jump out of his skin with fright, but it only lasted a few seconds, because he recognized the rascally rascal, MOOC, and had to laugh at all his ruses. He did so now.

Perhaps it was the quick nap or perhaps it was the scare, but his head felt clear. Nowhere in sight were any peyote emeralds. Thus, gone too were his hallucinations. No one save the dog and MOOC remained. Whether all those people had actually been here, he was not certain. What he was certain of, though, was that he was again one with nature. He took a breath of fresh air and felt the breeze in his hair and smelt the sap of wood in the air. To him, this was heaven.

The dog barked playfully. He responded by saying, "Hippie is here to play, so come, Pup." The dog was no puppy since he weighed half his weight and was nearly his height when he toppled Hippie over, but there was no ferociousness in the dog's eyes. Hippie was a good judge of all animals and nature.

They wrestled with innocent fun. They jabbed and tackled and play fought, but at no time did the dog come close to hurting Hippie nor vice versa. Even MOOC joined in his own way, scratching, jumping, and clawing nearby, but not actually touching anyone. They were all quick friends, no matter what the previous relations between MOOC and the dog had been. But soon the playful games finished. The Rottweiler and marten went back to their respective homes; both would probably sleep for a long time after such a hectic morning.

So, he was left totally alone—how Hippie often liked it. He decided to take the opportunity to walk, explore, and think—always refreshing, always enlightening. And when he was in Wyoming, especially Yellowstone Park, he did his best contemplations.

All the events that had taken place since he left that roof in California had been entertaining at times and exulting at others. But no matter if he had slummed in a truck with Maude, been worshipped by

Bearman, gone waterskiing as Aspen, been questioned by a fake reporter turned succubus, or had been drugged by peyote emeralds, it was all good. Adventure just happened, as did always ending up in Wyoming. But tranquility and happiness were a true state of mind. Whatever happened on the outside, he would always have that inner peace, and he would always work at staying healthy.

These thoughts reminded him of a devised word he sometimes like to use: "*Ridicula*". To him the word meant: *ridiculous to most but par for the course for the selected few*, which included him, of course. He did realize that ridícula meant ridiculous in Spanish, but his own English translation of the word suited him just fine.

He walked through the woods as the sun brought unusually hot weather for this time of year. That had to do with climate change he was sure, but right now he didn't worry about that, preferring to revel in the warmth and live for the moment.

Because that's what everything was about. Wherever he was, he would do his best to help animals and nature or at least not disturb them, but he was about the here and now: whatever happens happens—let nature take its course. In other words, there didn't need to be any major development, catastrophe, alien invasion, or likewise to find enlightenment. Wisdom was the best enlightenment, and he hoped everyone he had met these last few days found that wisdom in their adventures.

He believed that they did, and everyone was better for it in their own way. He had to believe that Jim really knew that Hippie was not Jesus, that George and Carolyn had found love, however weird their relationship, that Maude would sell her peyote emeralds, petrified timber, and an assortment of KIDS products for both prosperity and the betterment of lives, and that the rest of the bunch found their way back home, ever the wiser with this sharing of adventure.

He came upon the Douglas-fir tree and rejoiced in its height and bulk and grace. A live Christmas tree in nature, never to be cut, not this one anyway. He knew instinctively that would be the case, especially since it lay in the protected Yellowstone Park. Hippie loved this place. He officially loved Wyoming. He loved niacin. He loved whatever came his way.

He loved.

Hippie walked on, realizing that he carried nothing, wore tattered clothes, and smelled like the wood that was his true namesake along with fir, leaves, dirt, and body odor. All of it blended into something more, something somehow fresh.

Nature and life.

He found his way to a house, more like a cabin really, with a neat garden in front and a welcoming porch. Here was the edge of civilization, probably just off a border of the park, for he hadn't been paying attention and probably had walked a distance away from any boundaries. Further beyond would be cars, stores, noise, and drudgery.

He preferred to stay where he was. He loved the nature around him, as he counted three doves flying directly in front of him followed by seven hummingbirds darting after them. Were those the same hummingbirds he had seen earlier?

From the house, a woman's voice yelled, "Harrison, you nitwit, you left the water running again!"

"Still brushing my teeth, dear," the man replied.

"I'm talking about the kitchen faucet."

"Oops," Hippie heard Harrison whimper from nearby.

"I'll turn off the faucet," a younger woman's voice said helpfully.

"Thank you, Dara. It's good to have you back to watch over him, if just for a few days," said the first woman's voice with much more calmness and care than before.

"Yes, thank you," added Harrison. Immediately afterward his voice changed cadences, and he shouted, "Pebbles! And Frecks, my splendid dog! Both you animals, get back here!"

"You too, my young pup, Rags. Come back," yelled the younger woman—Dara.

A cat ran out followed by two dogs, both dogs barking in joyful pursuit, not really trying to catch the tabby. Hippie recognized one of the dogs immediately: the Rottweiler. *Awesome!*

Yes, this cabin and its inhabitants would be hospitable to him. No question. Nebraska could wait for his arrival a while longer.

For this night, he would sleep on the roof. Because staying ridicula suited him just fine.

Epilogue

Exactly twenty years from the moment Hippie, the boy ranger, and Maude exited the clubhouse consisting of Maude's collectible riches, a green evanescence glimmers in an otherwise empty space. Long since had the place been abandoned; even the boy ranger had grown up and forgotten about the place, which now stood dilapidated, almost in ruin, but still somehow remained upright. Maude had emptied the clubhouse a long time ago of nearly all her treasures, save the one.

That one peyote emerald now gleams from within a tiny crevice that even the squirrels had never found. It had laid dormant for all the twenty years that Maude had taken to establish her empire of peyote emeralds and clothing, petrified timber, and useless junk that consumers ate up, because people know no better except to follow fads and make the corporate and avaricious world richer. The biggest fad of the moment is shoes, always in fashion in some way, and since Jade, who had become the latest person to be famous for being famous, sported three-inch petrified wooden emerald shoes, everyone is buying them.

But greed is not Maude's purpose at all, for the emeralds and timber had another value besides getting people high and keeping campfires flourishing for as long as a night persists. This value lay in the fact that the two products coexisting together chemically, originally combined in Maude's labs, produced clean air. Thus, the mix of emeralds and timber spaced systematically across large land areas in the form of laced clothes, jewelry, trinkets, and other crap benefited millions, and they did not know it.

Her corporation, which now controlled Wyoming with government approval, had, in effect—with thousands of employees who did a lot of hard work (some of which involved continuously planting new trees)—become a separate entity all to itself and had significant holdings all the way to Vancouver. Thus, despite the inept government and ugly corporate politics that still insisted that pollution and climate change were good fiction, nature in Wyoming flourishes. Plants emit fresh oxygen, flowers blossom, animals—led by the descendants of Freckles, the Great Rottweiler—prosper, and the Douglas-fir still stands above it all, protected by the descendants of MOOC.

The coming to life of the peyote emerald that controlled the entire network is a significant event that almost no one knows anything about. Its light signified that all is well in Yellowstone Park and the surrounding areas.

Finally.

Hippie sees that light from where he sits a few meters away, for he has been called back to Wyoming yet again to witness the radiance. He is older but has not changed in personality, for Hippie still loves being a New-Age hippy, sporting a long brown healthy beard and some tattered clothes, and Aspen still comes forward to play. In his fifties, he remains vibrant.

He brings forth a capsule of niacin and swallows it. He doesn't care if it mixed with the peyote from the emerald to produce strong holistic hallucinations, because that would feel great!

For the first time that day, he observes his welcomed companions: Kenny and Maria, now married, join him in his celebration of the emerald, while their pilot, Bobarino, waits for them by his craft (the original hot air balloon pilot has yet to return to this spot). The couple takes their niacin, kiss, and watch as the radiance of the emerald glows.

Hippie does have one disappointment. George and Carolyn could not join him for this momentous reunion. As matter of fact, none of them have ever seen them again after that fateful day twenty years ago. Jim had prayed for them but that was unnecessary. They are fine. They have joined the living underworld: whether in reality or not, Hippie isn't certain. But he does know that George and Carolyn had totally fallen in love, remain so to this day, and would stay that way forever, perhaps literally. *Crazy love. Blood soulmates!*

And then the light of the emerald extinguishes. It has shown its health and would hopefully do so again in another twenty years.

Hippie rises and smiles. He's free, he's happy, he has friends, and he's healthy.

That's all he has ever needed.

About the Author

Growing up in Woodstock, NY, Adam Altman has been exposed to the creative arts for his entire life. His fiction books include his fantasy novels, set in the Land of Tasmear, which began with LifeShaker and continues with Dream Spells. His Liliana young adult novels include Liliana's Fan and the final book in the series, Liliana's Realms. He also has written acclaimed poetry and a children's picture book, entitled The Frog's Golden Water. Ridicula is a departure for him, because it is neither from the fantasy nor children/young adult genres. Instead, this book is humorous fiction and is highly metaphorical, covering themes dear to his heart.

More details about his works can be found at www.Tasmear.com.

Other Books by Adam Altman

Tasmear Series
LifeShaker
Dream Spells

Liliana Series
Liliana's Fan
Liliana's Summer
Liliana & Felip
Liliana's Realms
Liliana (Omnibus of all 4 novels)

Enlightened Darkness
The Frog's Golden Water

www.ingramcontent.com/pod-product-compliance
Lightning Source LLC
Chambersburg PA
CBHW030323080526
44584CB00012B/683